Congratulations on taking this exciting step towards a rewarding career in Sterile Processing! I'm confident that the Sterile Processing Mentorship Academy E-Test Workbook/E-Study Guide will be an invaluable tool on your journey.

This is more than just a book; it's an investment in your future. As you delve into the world of sterilization, decontamination, and infection prevention, remember that you're not just learning about instruments and techniques – you're becoming an essential guardian of patient safety.

The knowledge and skills you gain will empower you to make a real difference in the lives of others. With dedication and perseverance, you'll be well on your way to a successful and fulfilling career in Sterile Processing. Embrace this opportunity and let your passion shine!

This is your calling! You were born to make a difference in this field. Don't let anything dim your fire, your passion, your drive. There will be challenges, absolutely. But within you lies the strength and resilience to overcome them all. Visualize your success, feel it in your heart, and let that be your guiding star. This is your journey, and you are destined to shine brightly. Now go out there and claim your victory!

Lastly, please utilize the position description below as a reference when developing your resume. Incorporating the terminology and concepts outlined will effectively communicate your qualifications and suitability for sterile processing positions. I hope this position description helps make your resume building a lot easier.

Renita Hoof

Clinical Director, ST, CRCST, CHL, CIS, CER, MRCST

The Sterile Processing Technician plays a critical role in ensuring patient safety and maintaining a high standard of care by providing sterile instruments and equipment to all departments within the healthcare facility. This position involves meticulous cleaning, decontamination, inspection, assembly, sterilization, and distribution of surgical instruments, medical devices, and equipment. The technician adheres to strict protocols and regulatory standards to prevent infection and ensure the functionality of all processed items.

Essential Duties and Responsibilities:

- **Decontamination and Sterilization:**
    - Prepare medical equipment and instruments for decontamination following established procedures.
    - Operate specialized equipment (e.g., ultrasonic cleaners, washers, sterilizers) to clean, disinfect, and sterilize instruments, devices, and equipment.
    - Adhere to all departmental policies and procedures related to decontamination and sterilization.
    - Maintain accurate records of sterilization cycles, including biological and chemical indicators.
- **Inspection and Assembly:**
    - Carefully inspect instruments and equipment for damage, wear, and functionality.
    - Assemble instrument trays and sets according to established procedures (e.g., using OneSource).
    - Prepare and package instruments and supplies for sterilization using appropriate wrapping techniques.
- **Inventory and Distribution:**
    - Unpack, check, and stock new equipment, instruments, and devices.

    - Maintain adequate inventory levels of sterile supplies and equipment.
    - Deliver equipment and supplies to various departments within the facility.
    - Respond promptly to emergency supply requests, particularly during surgical procedures.
- **Quality Control and Safety:**
    - Monitor temperature and humidity conditions within storage areas to ensure the integrity of sterile items.
    - Participate in quality assurance activities and departmental audits.
    - Adhere to all safety regulations and infection control standards (OSHA, CDC, AAMI, AORN).
    - Report any damaged or malfunctioning equipment to the appropriate personnel.
- **Collaboration and Communication:**
    - Communicate effectively with operating room staff to ensure the availability of required instruments.
    - Collaborate with the Materials Department to maintain appropriate stock levels.
    - Maintain professional and courteous interactions with all healthcare staff.

Knowledge, Skills, and Abilities:

- **Technical Knowledge:**
    - Thorough understanding of sterilization principles and techniques.
    - Knowledge of surgical instruments and medical equipment.
    - Familiarity with infection control procedures and safety standards.

    - Ability to operate and troubleshoot sterile processing equipment.
- **Analytical Skills:**
    - Ability to inspect instruments for damage and wear.
    - Attention to detail in assembling instrument sets and maintaining accurate records.
- **Physical Abilities:**
    - Ability to lift and move trays of instruments and equipment weighing up to 25 lbs.
    - Ability to stand, walk, and bend for extended periods.
    - Manual dexterity and tactile differentiation.
- **Communication and Interpersonal Skills:**
    - Effective communication and interpersonal skills.
    - Ability to work collaboratively in a fast-paced environment.

Questions and Answers.

Please research the "why". It will help you to know the answer no matter how the question is worded on the exam.

1) A case cart pick list contains information that:

a. Assist the surgeon during the procedure.
b. Is used to assemble surgical instrument sets.
c. **Identifies the supplies, utensils and instruments needed for a specific procedure.**

Explain Why:

____

____

____

2) SPD workflow should move from dirty to clean. True/False

Explain Why:

____

____

____

3) Which of the following would be the best choice for high-level disinfection of instruments?

a. Phenolics
b. Chlorine
c. Iodophors
d. Ortho-phthalaldehyde (OPA)

Explain Why:

____

____

____

4) Following the steam sterilization process, which of the following is NOT a factor of cooling time?

a. Size of package
b. Time it is needed for a procedure
c. Type of packaging used
d. Temperature and humidity of the room

Explain Why:

____

____

____

5) The end of a body part of an endoscope that is farthest away from the point of origin or the end of an instrument that is farthest away from the operator is called the _____end.

a. Lateral
b. Distal
c. Proximal
d. Medical

Explain Why:

____

____

____

6) The suffix -ectomy means:

a. To repair
b. <u>Surgical removal</u>
c. Inflammation
d. To cut

Explain Why:

____

____

____

7) Which solution is known to damage surgical instrumentation?

a. Betadine
b. <u>Saline water</u>
c. Critical water
d. Enzymatic spray

Explain Why:

____

____

____

8) The suffix - tome means:

a. Surgical restoration
b. Surgical fixation
c. To suture
d. <u>A cutting instrument</u>

Explain Why:

____

____

____

9) Soiled instruments are received in the _____area of SPD.

a. Preparation
b. Packaging
c. Decontamination
d. Sterilization

Explain Why:

____

____

____

10) Devices that are introduced directly into the bloodstream or other normally sterile areas of the body are classified as:

a. Critical devices
b. Semi critical devices
c. Non-critical devices
d. Critical care equipment

Explain Why:

____

____

____

11) How often should a steam sterilizer door gasket be inspected and wiped clean?

a. Daily
b. Weekly

c. Monthly
d. Every two months

Explain Why: Explain Why:

___

___

___

12) How should sterile packages be arranged and maintained to allow for stock rotation?

a. Take from the bottom first
b. Last in, first out
c. First in, first out
d. Last in, last out

Explain Why:

___

___

___

13) The floors in decon should be:

a. Wet mopped daily
b. Wet mopped weekly
c. Swept daily and wet mopped weekly
d. Swept daily

Explain Why:

___

___

___

14) Which of the following instruments has teeth?

a. <u>Tissue forceps</u>
b. Needle holders
c. Chisels
d. Osteotomes

<u>Explain Why:</u>

____

____

____

15) Which steps occur first when processing a flexible scope?

a. <u>Leak testing</u>
b. High-level disinfection
c. Manual cleaning
d. Drying

<u>Explain Why:</u>

____

____

____

16) What information is *not* required on the label of a sterilized package?

a. Description of package contents
b. Lot control number
c. <u>Surgeon identification</u>
d. Identification of sterilizer and cycle to be used

<u>Explain Why:</u>

____

____

____

17) The best way to clean a suction lumen is:

a. Using warm water running water
b. <u>Using the proper-sized brush</u>
c. Soaking in an enzymatic solution for three minutes
d. Using the appropriate stylet

<u>Explain Why:</u>

____

____

____

18) When placing sterile items on the shelf, check:

a. Package integrity
b. Expiration date
c. Seals and filters to confirm they are intact
d. <u>All the above</u>

<u>Explain Why:</u>

____

____

____

19) How long can flexible endoscopes that have undergone HLD or liquid chemical sterilization be stored?

a. One week
b. One month
c. Six weeks

d. According to the facility policy

Explain Why:

____

____

____

20) The decontamination area should have:

a. Negative airflow
b. Positive airflow
c. Filtered airflow
d. No air is exchanged because it is a hazardous area

Explain Why:

____

____

____

21) Information about chemical or hazardous substances must be:

a. Available to all employees
b. Locked in a storage cabinet
c. Locked in the manager's office
d. Kept only with the facility's safety officer

Explain Why:

____

____

____

22) Which of the following is a professional organization consisting of perioperative nurses and others dedicated to providing optimal care to the surgical patient?

a. AAMI
b. AORN
c. APIC
d. ISO

Explain Why:

____

____

____

23) What does ORIF stand for Open Reduction Internal Fixation

Explain Why:

____

____

24) What does BSO stand for Bilateral salpingo-oophorectomy

Explain Why:

____

____

25) What does BKA stand for: Below Knee Amputation

Explain Why:

____

____

26) What does TAH stand for Total Abdominal Hysterectomy

Explain Why:

____

____

27) What does CABG stand for Coronary artery bypass graft

Explain Why:

____

____

28) Does CR stand for Closed Reduction

Explain Why:

____

____

29) The prefix hyper-mean? Above, excessive

Explain Why:

____

____

30) The prefix inter- means? Between

Explain Why:

____

____

31) The amount of time an item must remain *wet* with a disinfectant to achieve disinfection is called:

a. Holding time

b. Wet contact time
c. Activation
d. Sterilization time

Explain Why:

____

____

32) The surgery that removes the uterus:

a. Hysteroscopy
b. Hysterectomy
c. Dilation and curettage
d. Bilateral salpingo-oophorectomy

Explain Why:

____

____

33) Arthroscopy instruments are used during:

a. Robotic surgery
b. Laparoscopic surgery
c. Joint surgery
d. All the above

Explain Why:

____

____

34) Devices listed as critical items must be ____ prior to use.

a. High level disinfected
b. Intermediate-level disinfected
c. Low-level disinfected

d. Sterilized

Explain Why:

____

____

35) Manual cleaning is the first step when reprocessing an endoscope. True or False - Leak Testing

Explain Why:

____

____

36) What area are ultrasonic machines used in?

a. Prep and assembly
b. Decontamination
c. Sterile Storage
d. Eye clinic

Explain Why:

____

____

____

37) The sterile storage process starts:

a) As soon as the sterilizer door is opened at the end of a cycle
b) As soon as the item leaves prep and assembly
c) As soon as the item enters the decontamination room
d) As soon as the SPD tech signs into the computer

Explain Why:

____

____

____

38) The difference between IUSS and a regular sterilization cycle:

a. Reduced dry cycle
b. No dry cycle
c. Longer exposure time
d. No exposure time

Explain Why:

____

____

____

39) The term -excise means:

a. Open
b. Close Reduction
c. Cut out
d. Look into

Explain Why:

____

____

40) HAIs (Healthcare-associated infections) are:

a. Infections that occur on or after day three of a hospitalization
b. Are the same as surgical site infections (SSI)
c. Caused by drug-resistant organisms
d. Expected

Explain Why:

____

____

41) If equipment becomes faulty during a procedure, the equipment should be:

a. Deemed unusable until the next procedure
b. OSHA (Occupational Safety and Health Administration should be contacted
c. Returned to Biomedical Department
d. Continue to be used

Explain Why:

____

____

42) Temperature and humidity levels should be monitored at least weekly in Sterile Processing. True or False

Explain Why:

____

____

43) Microbes:

a. Are useful for breaking down sewage
b. Can produce toxins
c. Can be useful in fluid products
d. All the above

Explain Why:

____

____

44) Case Cart Systems:

a. It is not necessary if there is a small facility
b. <u>Reduce the amount of space needed for supply storage in user departments</u>
c. Are an automated doctor preference generator
d. Require duplicate cart of supplies in inventory

<u>Explain Why:</u>

____

____

46) Wrapped instrument sets should not be stacked because:

a. It causes the shelving to bow
b. <u>It can cause possible holes in the wrapper</u>
c. Staff doesn't know how to stack appropriately
d. Trays may become damaged

<u>Explain Why:</u>

____

____

47) The suffix -plasty means:

a. To excise
b. <u>Surgical restoration</u>
c. To remove
d. To create an opening

<u>Explain Why:</u>

____

____

48) Using untreated water in decontamination:

a. Increases the likelihood of mineral deposits on instruments
b. Causes patient delays
c. Recommended in the Safety Data Sheet
d. Recommended in Competency Check Sheet

Explain Why:

____

____

49) Sterile Trays should be:

a. Lifted, not dragged
b. Weigh 25 lbs or less
c. Untouched until they are cooled properly
d. All the above

Explain Why:

____

____

50) To minimize the exposure to bloodborne pathogens and other bio-hazardous contaminant, Sterile Processing technicians must wear special attire referred to as:

a. Gowns
b. Gloves
c. Personal safety attire
d. Personal Protective Equipment

Explain Why:

____

____

51) Which is not a goal for pre cleaning of reusable medical equipment:

a. Removing contaminants and biofilm
b. Preventing cross-contamination
c. Preventing damage to instrumentation during procedure and transportation
d. Transporting instruments within an hour after the procedure ended

Explain Why:

52) The FDA classifies sterilization packaging as a:

a. Class VI medical device
b. Class II medical device
c. Class III medical device
d. Class I medical device

Explain Why:

53) The term ostomy is a:

a. Prefix
b. Suffix
c. Root word
d. None of the above

Explain Why:

54) Instrument inspection is completed:

a. After cleaning
b. Before cleaning
c. After use
d. After sterilization

Explain Why:

____

____

55) Which type of packaging system can be used for IUSS?

a. Paper/plastic pouches
b. Glass material
c. Tyvek pouches
d. Containers that have been validated for IUSS by the manufacturer

Explain Why:

____

____

56) When is the Point of Use treatment performed?

a. Immediately when the set has entered into decontamination
b. Immediately after the procedure
c. Immediately during assembly
d. None of the above

Explain Why:

____

____

57) The basic unit of a living organism is a:

a. <u>Cell</u>
b. Organ
c. Heart
d. Lung

<u>Explain Why:</u>

____

____

58) The largest part of the human brain is the:

a. <u>Cerebrum</u>
b. Skull
c. Brain Stem
d. Cerebellum

<u>Explain Why:</u>

____

____

59) Survey readiness is the responsibility of:

a. Sterile Processing Technicians
b. Sterile Processing Director
c. Surgical Staff
d. <u>Everyone's responsibility</u>

<u>Explain Why:</u>

____

____

60) The human ear is made up of three parts:

a. External, middle, and eardrum
b. Funnel, stapes, and malleus
c. Inner, middle, and external
d. Stapes, sclera and inner

Explain Why:

____

____

61) The Joint Commission (TJC) requires that preventative maintenance (PM) standards be established for medical devices.

a. True
b. False

Explain Why:

____

____

62) Thermal disinfection is accomplished using:

a. Prolonged steam pressure
b. Heated chemicals
c. Heated glutaraldehyde
d. Heat

Explain Why:

____

____

63) Dynamic air removal is how steam flush pressure pulse sterilizers are classified.

a. True
b. False

Explain Why:

____

____

64) Tuberculosis is an example of a fungus.

a. True
b. False

Explain Why:

____

____

65) Asepsis is defined as the absence of microorganisms.

a. True
b. False

Explain Why:

____

____

67) Capital equipment are large ticket items with a high purchase price. Name this type of equipment.

a. Sterilizer
b. Stapler

c. Keyboard
d. None of above

Explain Why:

____

____

68) External Chemical Indicators (CI) are found on the outside of containers or packages.

a. True
b. False

Explain Why:

____

____

69) Hand hygiene should be performed:

a. Before leaving work
b. After eating
c. Before starting
d. All the above

Explain Why:

____

____

70) All patient care equipment that is received after use must be considered contaminated and handled as such regardless of its appearance.

a. True

b. False

Explain Why:

____

____

71) How long must alcohol remain in wet contact with an item to achieve a reasonable level of disinfection?

a. One to four minutes
b. Two to four minutes
c. <u>Five to ten minutes</u>
d. 10-15 minutes

Explain Why:

____

____

72) Instruments should be manually cleaned using what type of method:

a. Stiff metal brush
b. Water enhanced spray
c. Round and round method
d. To and fro motion

Explain Why:

____

____

73) Instrument sets that overhang on the shelf are prone to become contaminated because:

a. <u>Possibility of falling on the floor</u>

b. Possibility of patient care issue
c. Possibility of wrong placement
d. None of the above

Explain Why:

74) What does this symbol mean 

a. Date of manufacturer
b. Expiration date
c. End-of-life date
d. None of the above

Explain Why:

75) What does this symbol mean 

a. Date of manufacturer
b. Expiration date
c. End-of-life date
d. None of the above

Explain Why:

76) What does this symbol mean 

a. Date of manufacturer
b. Product can not be resterilized
c. Product can not be submerged
d. None of the above

77) The inventory system uses preference cards:

a. Par level system
b. Exchange cart system
c. Case Cart System
d. Requisition

Explain Why:

____

____

78) Both the Association of periOperative Registered Nurses (AORN) and The Joint Commission (TJC) both recommend that Immediate Use Steam Sterilization (IUSS) be decreased.

a. True
b. False

Explain Why:

____

____

79) Which system provides supplies and instruments for surgical cases?

a. Inventory
b. Case cart

c. Exchange cart
d. Requisition

Explain Why:

____

____

80) Endoscopes are NOT time-consuming to reprocess.

a. True
b. False

Explain Why:

____

____

81) Which are the following locations not ideal for sterile storage?

a. Next to or near an outside hallway
b. In a regulated temperature area
c. Inside of Sterile Processing
d. None of the above

Explain Why:

____

____

82) The purpose of a combining vowel:

a. Give the primary meaning of a word
b. Make words easier to pronounce
c. Connect vowels and root words
d. All of the above

Explain Why:

____

____

83) What does the “Rachet” do on an instrument

a. Lock it into place
b. Close it
c. Crevice
d. Intricate

Explain Why:

____

____

84) The floors of the Decontamination area should be cleaned:

a. Weekly
b. Daily
c. When requested
d. After a spill only

Explain Why:

____

____

85) The floors in the storage area should be cleaned:

a. Weekly
b. Daily
c. When requested
d. None of the above

Explain Why:

____

____

86) All floors in sterile processing should be cleaned with a broom:

a. True
b. False

Explain Why:

____

____

87) Lighting is not an essential part of sterile processing:

a. True
b. False

Explain Why:

____

____

88) What are the minimum air exchanges in the decontamination area:

a. 5 per hour
b. 10 per hour
c. 15 per hour
d. Minimum of 10, depending on how large the room is

Explain Why:

____

____

89) What does the acronym AER stand for:

a. Automated endoscope reprocessor
b. Automated ear reprocessor
c. Automated entry reprocessor
d. None of the above

Explain Why:

____

____

90) Washer disinfector screens should be cleaned:

a. Daily
b. Weekly
c. Monthly
d. Doesn't need cleaning

Explain Why:

____

____

91) Ultrasonic machines use cavitation for:

a. Cleaning
b. Disinfecting
c. Sterilization
d. Alcohol bath

Explain Why:

____

____

92) The absence of microorganisms is called:

a. Asepsis
b. Infection prevention and control
c. Hospital Acquired Infection
d. Surgical Site Infection

Explain Why:

____

____

93) A Bowie Dick test is a *Class III* (CI) that is cleared by the US Food and Drug Administration (FDA) and runs daily in dynamic air removal sterilizers.

a. True
b. False

Explain Why:

____

____

94) A Class II Bowie Dick test is run at the beginning of each day before each load to determine if the sterilizer dynamic air removal mechanism is working correctly in the sterilizer.

a. True
b. False

Explain Why:

____

____

95) An instrument with a shiny surface is known to have a "MIRROR" Finish.

a. True
b. False

Explain Why:

____

____

96) The surgical procedure that removes the uterus:

a. Hysterectomy
b. Dilation and Curettage
c. Bilateral salpingo-oophorectomy
d. Laparoscopic arthroscopy

Explain Why:

____

____

97) The drain screen inside of the sterilizer must be cleaned:

a. Daily
b. Weekly
c. Monthly
d. Doesn't need cleaning

Explain Why:

____

____

98) What is the preferred pH balance used for most detergent and cleaning processes?

a. Low pH
b. Foaming pH
c. <u>Neutral pH</u>
d. High pH

<u>Explain Why:</u>

____

____

98) What is the pH level that is less than 7 called:

a. <u>Acidic</u>
b. Alkaline
c. Neutral
d. None of the above

<u>Explain Why:</u>

____

____

99) What is the pH level that is greater than 7:

a. <u>Alkaline</u>
b. Acidic
c. Neutral
d. None of the above

<u>Explain Why:</u>

100) The procedure to remove the stomach is:

a. Endoscopic stomach removal
b. Gastrectomy
c. Gastric bypass
d. Gastritis

Explain Why:

101) When removing PPE what should be removed first?

a. Bonnet
b. Mask
c. Gloves
d. Shoe covers

Explain Why:

102) The decontamination room is a negative room:

a. True
b. False

Explain Why:

____

103) The sterile storage area is a positive room:

a. True
b. False

Explain Why:

____

____

104) To prevent aerosolization all items should be brushed below water level:

a. True
b. False

Explain Why:

____

____

105) What color stain is gram-positive bacteria?

a. Blue
b. Light blue
c. Purple
d. Yellow

Explain Why:

____

____

106) The measure of acidity and or alkalinity refers to:

a. Gram stain
b. Humidity
c. pH level
d. Water temperature

Explain Why:

____

____

107) Neutral pH level is:

a. 7
b. 14
c. 10
d. 8

Explain Why:

____

____

108) pH levels range from 0-14

a. True
b. False

Explain Why:

____

____

109) Understanding anatomy assist sterile processing technicians to:

a. Understand how to clean instruments
b. Understand how to sterilize instruments

c. Understand the parts of the body where instruments are used
d. Understand how to use it in surgery

Explain Why:

____

____

110) Hypoglycemia means:

a. Low blood sugar
b. High blood sugar
c. Low liver functions
d. High liver functions

Explain Why:

____

____

111) Biohazardous materials are received in which area of sterile processing:

a. Prep and pack area
b. Soiled utility room
c. Decontamination area
d. Storage area

Explain Why:

____

____

112) Microbiology is the study of:

a. Cells
b. Life
c. <u>Microorganisms</u>
d. None of the above

<u>Explain Why:</u>

____

____

113) Cleaning ophthalmic instruments should be done in a:

a. Dedicated sink
b. Dedicated eye ultrasonic
c. Dedicated ophthalmic detergent
d. <u>All the above</u>

<u>Explain Why:</u>

____

____

114) Subcutaneous means:

a. <u>Beneath the skin</u>
b. Cut on the skin
c. Tissue
d. Joint

<u>Explain Why:</u>

____

____

115) Microorganisms are capable of forming a thick wall around themselves, enabling them to survive in adverse conditions:

a. Cells
b. Colonization
c. Nuclei
d. Spores

Explain Why:

116) Detergents used in ultrasonic washers and cart washers should be:

a. Low foaming
b. High foaming
c. Interchangeable
d. Clear in color

Explain Why:

117) The Association of periOperative Registered Nurses (AORN) is:

a. The professional organization that writes guidelines for the Operating Room
b. The professional organization that writes guidelines for the Sterile Processing Department
c. The professional organization that writes guidelines for the Decontamination area
d. The professional organization that writes guidelines for The Joint Commission

Explain Why:

---

118) Doffing of PPE means to:

a. Take off
b. Put on
c. Leave on
d. None of the above

Explain Why:

---

119) Donning of PPE means to:

a. Take off
b. Put on
c. Leave on
d. None of the above

Explain Why:

---

120) What is the critical first step before instruments enter decontamination?

a. Precleaning
b. Washing
c. Decontamination
d. Infection Prevention

Explain Why:

____

____

Research the following questions and answer below:

121) What should be worn when handling biohazard waste?

Answer and Explain Why:

____

____

122) How often should brushes be discarded?

Answer and Explain Why:

____

____

123) In your own words describe what pitting means.

Answer and Explain Why:

____

____

124) What type of brush is prohibited in Decontamination?

Answer and Explain Why:

____

125) How many Spaulding Classifications are there?

Answer:

126) What does TASS stand for?

Answer:

127) Name a type of instrument/equipment that correlates to each of the Spaulding Classifications.

Answer:

128) What makes pitted instruments difficult to clean?

Answer:

129) Eye Instruments can be manually cleaned in a normal workflow?

a. True
b. False

Explain Why:

130) What is the pH level of the detergent used for eye instruments?

Explain Why:

131) What type of signage should be placed on the outside of a container containing soiled containments?

a. Decontamination sticker
b. Biohazard sticker
c. Do not use sticker
d. No sticker needed

Explain Why:

132) Is dry mopping allowed in Decon?

Explain Why:

133) Are pitted instruments safe to use on a patient?

Explain Why:

134) What is the temperature in the decontamination area?

a. <u>60-65 degrees</u>
b. 70-75 degrees
c. 64-74 degrees
d. 55-65 degrees

<u>Explain Why:</u>

135) Pseudomonas aeruginosa is identified by which bacterial shape?

a. <u>Rod</u>
b. Spiral
c. Circle
d. Spherical

<u>Explain Why:</u>

136) When putting on PPE, which item should be put on first?

a. Mask
b. Gloves
c. <u>Gown</u>
d. It doesn't matter

<u>Explain Why:</u>

137) Which governing body conducts onsite surveys of healthcare facilities?

a. The Joint Commission
b. AORN
c. OSHA
d. The Society of Gastroenterology Nurses and Associates (SGNA)

Explain Why:

138) Sterile Processing Technicians should learn medical terminology to:

a. List surgical terms in healthcare setting
b. Assist SPD technicians to read doctors preference cards
c. Assist with understanding Safety Data Sheet (SDS)
d. Assist SPD technicians to prived the OR and medical team with goods and services needed without delay

Explain Why:

139) This classification system is used to categorize patient care items based on the degree of risk of infection:

a. Medical Device Classification
b. Reusable Medical Equipment Classification
c. Spaulding Classification
d. High Level Classification

Explain Why:

140) Mushrooms, yeast and mold are:

a. <u>Fungi</u>
b. Gram-negative
c. Gram-positive
d. None of Above

<u>Explain Why:</u>

141) Count sheets are:

a. Used only for OR personnel
b. <u>Used to describe instrumentation details in set</u>
c. Used for easy access for inventory
d. All of the above

<u>Explain Why:</u>

142) Which system gives the body its shape and support?

a. Nervous
b. <u>Skeletal</u>
c. Circulatory
d. Muscular

<u>Explain Why:</u>

143) How many bones make up the skeletal system?

a. 206
b. 210
c. 202
d. 200

Explain Why:

144) Pasteurizers disinfect using:

a. Phenols
b. Peracetic acid
c. Heated water
d. Pasteurized water

Explain Why:

145) An osteotome is used to:

a. Retract
b. Cut or shave bone
c. Hemostasis
d. None of the above

Explain Why:

146) To properly dry lumens and channels:

a. Use a syringe to push air through channels
b. Use the correct size brush to brush dry
c. Place instrument on drying towel
d. Use instrument air machine to force air out of lumens

Explain Why:

147) Surgery of the ear that reconstructs the eardrum that enables sound waves to be sent to the middle ear is:

a. Stapedectomy
b. Tympanoplasty
c. Myringotomy
d. Inner ear

Explain Why:

148) Pneumatic hoses should be:

a. Pressurized for proper inspection
b. Inspected using a microscope
c. Inspected using a borescope
d. All of the above

Explain Why:

149) MEC stands for what:

Explain Why:

150) Kerrison and laminectomy rongeurs should be tested using:

a. Paper towels
b. Rubber testing material
c. Index card
d. Sharpening block

Explain Why:

151) The prefix hemi- means:

a. Half
b. Between
c. Beyond
d. After

Explain Why:

152) Reusable Medical Equipment that categorize as semi- critical must be at least _____before use:

a. Sterilized
b. Low- level disinfected
c. <u>High Level disinfected</u>
d. Wiped off with alcohol

Explain Why:

____

____

153) The term septorhinoplasty refers to the nose:

a. <u>True</u>
b. False

Explain Why:

____

____

154) Testing of Laparoscopic instrument's insulation should be completed:

a. In Decontamination
b. In Surgery Suite
c. <u>In assembly area before set assembly</u>
d. During precleaning

Explain Why:

____

____

155) Who is OSHA and what do they assist the healthcare worker with:

Explain Why:

___

___

156) Arthroscopy instruments refers to:

a. Laparoscopic instruments
b. Joint surgery
c. Arthritis
d. Robotic surgery

Explain Why:

___

___

157) Chemical indicators are:

a. FDA Class I devices
b. FDA Class II devices
c. Spaulding Classification- Critical
d. Spaulding Classification- Semi Critical

Explain Why:

___

___

158) Musculoskeletal disorders refer to disorders of the muscle, nerves, tendons or joints.

a. True
b. False

Explain Why:

____

____

159) Biocidal is the process or ability to kill or control the growth of living organisms:

a. <u>True</u>
b. False

<u>Explain Why:</u>

____

____

160) The dress code apply to:

a. Sterile Processing Staff only
b. Engineering staff
c. Visitors
d. <u>Every one who enters the department</u>

<u>Explain Why:</u>

____

____

161) Laminectomy means:

a. Removal of tumor
b. <u>Removal of part of the vertebrae in the spine</u>
c. The study of the spine
d. All of the above

<u>Explain Why:</u>

____

162) Contaminated items may be returned to sterile processing in:

a. Solid container
b. Case cart
c. Container with biohazard sticker on it
d. <u>All of the above</u>

<u>Explain Why:</u>

163) Personal electronics such as cell phones should not be taken into sterile processing because they harbor microorganisms:

a. <u>True</u>
b. False

<u>Explain Why:</u>

165) The organization that regulates if medical devices are safe:

a. <u>FDA</u>
b. OSHA
c. AORN
d. AMMI

<u>Explain Why:</u>

166) Container rigid filter retention plate should be cleaned:

a. Together
b. <u>Separately</u>
c. Left attached
d. Not cleaned at all

<u>Explain Why:</u>

____

____

167) Decontamination staff should wear:

a. Fluid resistant gowns
b. Impervious gloves
c. Bonnet
d. <u>All the above</u>

<u>Explain Why:</u>

____

____

168) The lining of the uterus is called:

a. <u>Endometrium</u>
b. Vagina
c. Labia
d. Inner wall

<u>Explain Why:</u>

____

____

169) When an item is found during assembly that has bioburden on it, staff should:

a. Wipe off in assembly
b. Ignore and allow sterilizer to kill contaminates
c. <u>Send the whole tray back to decontamination area</u>
d. Only set the one item back to decontamination area

<u>Explain Why:</u>

____

____

170) During the decontamination process, the precleaning spray should not be washed off before placing set into detergent water.

a. True
b. <u>False</u>

<u>Explain Why:</u>

____

____

171) The first step in sterilization in the Sterile Processing Department is:

a. Precleaning
b. Packaging
c. <u>Decontamination</u>
d. High Level Disinfection

<u>Explain Why:</u>

____

____

172) The first step in sterilization before instrument reaches Sterile Processing is:

a. Transportation
b. <u>Precleaning</u>
c. Biohazard Signage
d. All of the above

Explain Why:

____

____

173) Sterile Processing workflow should begin:

a. Clean to sterile
b. <u>Soiled to clean</u>
c. Soiled to sterile
d. All the above

Explain Why:

____

____

174) A job description is the same as job duty list:

a. True
b. <u>False</u>

Explain Why:

____

____

175) Medical Devices are regulated by:

a. EPA
b. OSHA
c. AORN
d. FDA

Explain Why:

____

____

176) EPA is the agency that imposes very strict labeling requirements on manufacturers of disinfectants.

a. True
b. False

Explain Why:

____

____

177) Powered surgical instruments such as drills:

a. Can be submerged for 10 min
b. Can not be submerged
c. Should be placed in the washer disinfector
d. Should be placed in the ultrasonic washer

Explain Why:

____

____

178) **Lipase enzymes** are used to breakdown fatty deposits on struments:

a. True
b. False

Explain Why:

____

____

179) Untreated water decreases the likelihood of mineral scale deposits:

a. True
b. False

Explain Why:

____

____

180) After changing the water in the ultrasonic machine, the machine must be degassed to prevent excess bubbles to reduce the energy of the cavitation process:

a. True
b. False

Explain Why:

____

____

181) The decontamination area should have______airflow in relation to other areas:

a. Positive

b. 30%-60%
c. 10 air exchanges
d. <u>Negative</u>

Explain Why:

____

____

182) _________ should be used to pre-rinse instruments to prevent coagulation of protein:

a. <u>Cool Water</u>
b. Hot Water
c. Pre-treatment
d. Detergent

Explain Why:

____

____

183) Ophthalmic instruments can go through the washer disinfector:

a. True
b. <u>False</u>

Explain Why:

____

____

184) All instrument sets that are placed in the washer disinfector should:

a. Be placed on the racks with room in between them to allow water to flow freely to each set

b. Be in an open position to allow water to reach the box locks
c. Lids removed to allow water to reach instrumentation
d. All of the above

Explain Why:

____

____

185) Cleaning and sterilization instructions should be written by:

a. The Joint Commission
b. FDA
c. EPA
d. Manufacturer of the device

Explain Why:

____

____

186) Ultrasonic cleaners:

a. Disinfects endoscopes
b. Cleans powered equipment
c. Uses cavitation to clean devices with lumens and hard to reach areas
d. First step in decontamination process

Explain Why:

____

____

187) Steam Sterilizers use _____to sterilize instruments.

a. Hydrogen Peroxide

b. Steam
c. Glutaraldehydes (OPA)
d. Thermal disinfection

Explain Why:

____

____

188) Items introduced into the bloodstream or other sterile parts of the body are:

a. Class I
b. Class II
c. Critical
d. Semi-Critical

Explain Why:

____

____

189) ________is the best chemical of choice to high-level disinfect a semi-critical instrument.

a. OPA
b. Phenolics
c. Alcohol
d. Chlorine

Explain Why:

____

____

190) Hepa filtered air is how semi-critical items that undergo high-level disinfection are dried.

a. True
b. False

Explain Why:

____

____

191) Quaternary ammonium compounds (Quats) are incompatible with soap.

a. True
b. False

Explain Why:

____

____

192) Nitrile gloves are worn when working with what kind of disinfectant:

a. Alcohol
b. OPA
c. Steam
d. None of the above

Explain Why:

____

____

192) Water temperature is the key source of disinfection in the washer disinfector:

a. True
b. False

Explain Why:

____

____

193)The use of heat to kill all microorganisms except for spores is called:

a. High Level heat
b. Thermal Heat
c. Thermal Disinfection
d. Sterilization

Explain Why:

____

____

194) Glutaraldehyde and OPA are classified as being high-level disinfectants.

a. True
b. False

Explain Why:

____

____

195) Low to intermediate level disinfectants are:

a. Phenolics
b. OPA
c. Low foam detergents

d. All of the above

Explain Why:

____

____

196) Tungsten Carbide scissors are usually identified by:

a. <u>Gold handles</u>
b. Delicate
c. Sharpness
d. Engravement

Explain Why:

____

____

197) All loaned instruments must first be:

a. Checked into sterile processing
b. Decontaminated
c. Sterilized before use
d. <u>All the above</u>

Explain Why:

____

____

198) One of the reasons why powered equipment doesn't always work:

a. Lack of battery power
b. <u>No preventative maintenance</u>
c. Operator error

d. Not clean

Explain Why:

____

____

199) What is the first step in reprocessing a flexible endoscope:

a. Pre-cleaning
b. Leak testing
c. Manual cleaning
d. Inspecting

Explain Why:

____

____

200) Pneumatic hoses should be pressurized for proper inspection:

a. True
b. False

Explain Why:

____

____

201) Batteries used with power equipment should be charged:

a. Before sterilization
b. During procedure
c. Before decontamination
d. All of the above

Explain Why:

____

____

202) Robotic instruments are reprocessed in the same manner as laparoscopic instruments:

a. True
b. False

Explain Why:

____

____

203) Sterile packages located in sterile storage should be arranged:

a. By alphabetical order
b. By doctors preference
c. First in First Out
d. Manufacturer Instructions

Explain Why:

____

____

204) Sterile Storage should have at least______positive air exchanges per hour:

a. 4
b. 6
c. 8
d. 10

Explain Why:

____

____

205) The floor of the cart washer should be cleaned:

a. Daily
b. Weekly
c. Monthly
d. It isn't necessary because it is cleaned when carts are being washed

Explain Why:

____

____

206) A physical monitor of the cart washer, washer disinfector, and is called a printout.

a. True
b. False

Explain Why:

____

____

207) The information on the monitoring records must be:

a. Legible
b. Obtainable
c. Accurate
d. All the above

Explain Why:

____

____

209) Sterilizer load records should contain the following:

a. Name of items on the load
b. Number of items on the load
c. Sterilization parameters of the load
d. <u>All of the above</u>

<u>Explain Why:</u>

____

____

210) If the load fails during sterilization:

a. All items must be resterilized
b. The load must be recalled immediately
c. Sterilizer records must indicate why the load failed
d. <u>All the above</u>

<u>Explain Why:</u>

____

____

211) External indicators are not important as long as the inside indicator has passed:

a. True
b. <u>False</u>

<u>Explain Why:</u>

____

212) Internal indicators are deemed usable if they don't completely pass:

a. True
b. False

Explain Why:

213) New employees and personnel who receive a new position should always receive formal training:

a. True
b. False

Explain Why:

214) Internal indicators are also known as chemical indicators (CI)

a. True
b. False

Explain Why:

215) Open shelf system leaves the sets the most vulnerable to contamination:

a. True

b. False

Explain Why:

____

____

216) The bottom of the shelf in the sterile storage area should be:

a. Solid shelving to protect sets during cleaning of the floor
b. 10 inches from the floor
c. Wet dusted routinely
d. <u>All the above</u>

Explain Why:

____

____

217) Wrapped instrument sets should not be stacked because:

a. Stacking causes holes
b. Sterilization tape may come off during stacking
c. Sets are easily contaminated due to holes
d. <u>All the above</u>

Explain Why:

____

____

218) **Hinged instruments:** Instruments like scissors, forceps, and clamps should be placed in the autoclave in an open position.

a. <u>True</u>
b. False

Explain Why:

____

____

219) Chemical Indicators (CI) are placed in all sets before sterilization.

a. True
b. False

Explain Why:

____

____

220) Genesis pan filters do not have to be checked for holes if they are coming directly out of the package and placed in the top/bottom of set.

a. True
b. False

Explain Why:

____

____

221) Sterilization tape is not an external indicator.

a. True
b. False

Explain Why:

____

____

222) Tamper Evident Seal locks are an example of an external chemical indicator.

a. True
b. False

Explain Why:

____

____

223) Shelves should be at least _____ inches below sprinkler heads to avoid interfering with their spray pattern in case of fire.

a. 10
b. 8
c. 18
d. 4

Explain Why:

____

____

225) Study the following **Prefixes**:

Hemi- half
Para- beside, near
Septo- dividing wall
Chole- bile
Ante- before
Anti- against
Dis- apart

Make notes here to help you remember the terms:

Endo- within
Hyper- above
Hypo- below, deficient
Inter- between

Make notes here to help you remember the terms:

Intra- within
Per- through
Post- after
Pre- before

Sub- under, beneath

Make notes here to help you remember the terms:

226) Study the following **root words**:

Procto- rectum
Broncho- bronchus
Endo- within (also can be used as a prefix)
Artery- artery
Hyster- uterus
Herni- rupture
Artho- joint
Colo- colon

Make notes here to help you remember the terms:

Crani- skull
Lipo- fat
Litho- stone
Mast- breast
Oopher- ovary

Make notes here to help you remember the terms:

Osteo- bone
Rhino- nose
Trachea- trachea
Stoma- opening
Cardio- heart
Cysto- bladder

Make notes here to help you remember the terms:

227) Study the following **suffixes**:
Algia- pain
Cide- kill
Emia- blood
Gram- record/image
Itis- inflammation
Cise- cut
Ectomy- surgically remove
Oscopy- visual examination and possible treatment of organ or joint
Ostomy- creation of an opening
Otomy- incision into an organ

Make notes here to help you remember the terms:

Pexy- surgical fixation
Plasty- surgical restoration
Necrosis- death of tissue
Ology- study of
Oma- tumor
Pathy- disease
Rrhage- flow (hemorrhage)
Rrhaphy- to suture (myorraphy- to suture a muscle wound)
Tome- a cutting instrument such as a dermatome

Make notes here to help you remember the terms:

228) Surgical procedure to relieve pressure on the median nerve in your wrist:

a. Carpal tunnel release
b. Digital release
c. Arthroscopy repair
d. None of the above

Explain Why:

229) Also known as a tympanotomy, is a surgical procedure where a small incision is made in the eardrum (tympanic membrane).

a. Eardrum release
b. Myringotomy
c. Ear tubes
d. All the above

Explain Why:

230) Removal of the undescended testicle is also known as:

a. Orchiopexy
b. Salpingo-oophorectomy
c. Vasectomy
d. All the above

Explain Why:

231) Para means:

a. Beside or near
b. Distal end
c. Closed off
d. None of the above

Explain Why:

232) The prefix hypo- means:

a. Below
b. Above
c. Large
d. None of the above

Explain Why:

233) Medical terminology comes from what origin:

a. French or Latin
b. Greek or Latin
c. Latin or English
d. Latin and English

Explain Why:

235) What are the three Spaulding Classifications?

a. Critical, Non-Critical, Sterilization
b. Class I, Class II, Class III
c. Critical, Semi-Critical, Non-Critical
d. All the above

Explain Why:

236) What is the part of the scope that holds the lens, light source, working channel, and air/water suction ports?

a. Control Body
b. Distal Tip
c. Boot
d. Light Source Guide Post

Explain Why:

237) The term septorhinoplasty means:

a. Surgical repair of the nose
b. Surgical repair of the throat
c. Surgical repair to remove cyst
d. Surgical repair of the bladder

Explain Why:

238) Arthroscopy means the visual examination of a joint:

a. True
b. False

Explain Why:

239) Lithotripsy means crushing of a stone:

a. True
b. False

Explain Why:

____

____

240) Viruses are smaller than bacteria:

a. True
b. False

Explain Why:

____

____

241) What is the most difficult to kill:

a. Spore
b. Bacteria
c. Fungus
d. Yeast

Explain Why:

____

____

242) The measure of pH refers to:

a. Alkalinity
b. Acidity

c. Both A and B
d. None of the above

Explain Why:

____

____

243) Acidity is a pH balance that is less than 7:

a. True
b. False

Explain Why:

____

____

244) Alkaline refers to a pH balance that is neutral:

a. True
b. False

Explain Why:

____

____

245) Microorganisms are reproduced by a process called binary fission.

a. True
b. False

Explain Why:

____

246) Which is not a common bacterial shape?

a. Cylindrical
b. Spherical
c. Rod
d. All the above

Explain Why:

247) The center of the cell is called:

a. Nucleus
b. Binary fission
c. Membrane
d. Gram

Explain Why:

248) Hands should washed for at least:

a. 10 seconds
b. 15 seconds
c. 20 seconds
d. 25 seconds

Explain Why:

246) Ebola has an incubation period that ranges from 2 to 21 days after exposure:

a. True
b. False

Explain Why:

247) Which one is not a gram-positive bacteria:

a. Klebsiella
b. Pseudomonas
c. Escherichia coli
d. All of the above

Explain Why:

248) 95% bacteria is not harmful to humans:

a. True
b. False

Explain Why:

249) The colors of biohazard containers are:

a. Red/ blue
b. Red/ yellow
c. Red/ green
d. <u>Red /orange</u>

<u>Explain Why:</u>

____

____

250) Fluid-resistant gowns are worn to protect Sterile Processing Technicians from splashes and spills located in:

a. <u>Decontamination area</u>
b. Prep and Assembly
c. Distribution
d. Sterilization

<u>Explain Why:</u>

____

____

Please remember that all instruments must be sterilized in the open position. The boxlock cant be closed.

<u>Anatomy of an instrument:</u>

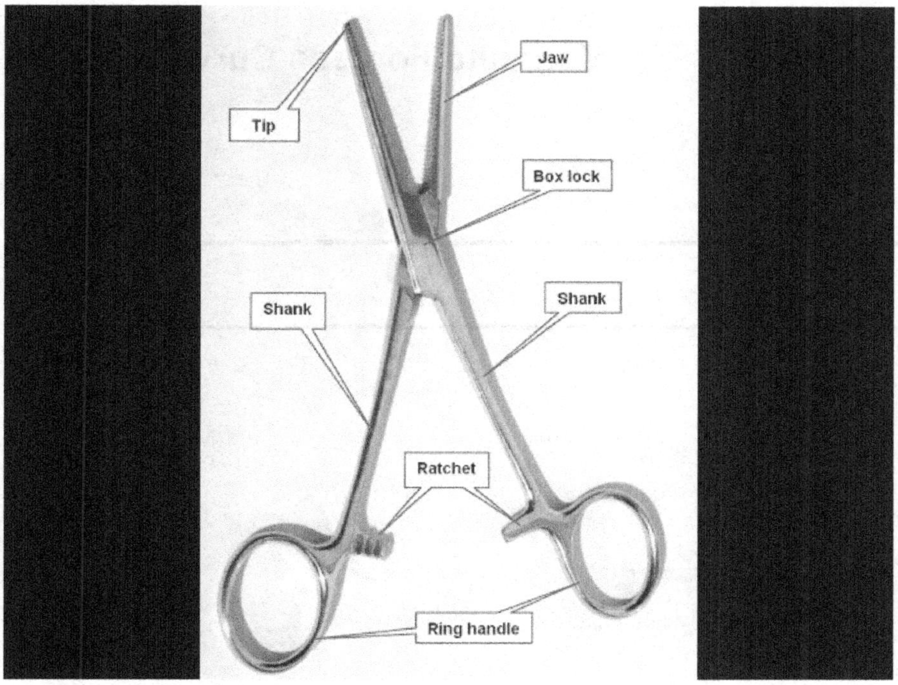

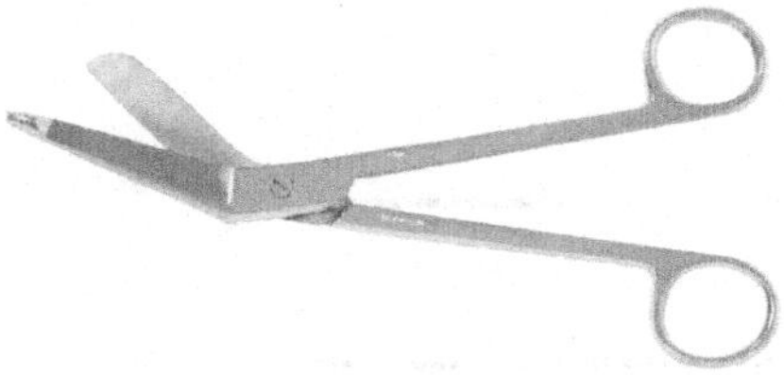

251) **Lister Bandage Scissors**

<u>Explain What It is Used For:</u>

____

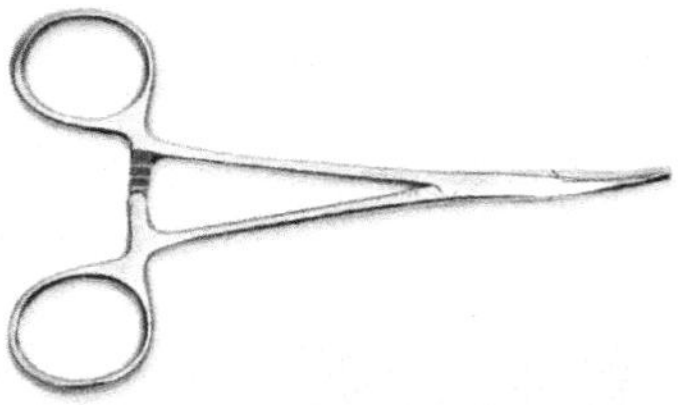

252) **Mosquito Forceps Curved**

Explain What It Is Used For:

____

____

253) **Adson Tissue Forceps**

Explain What It Is Used For:

____

____

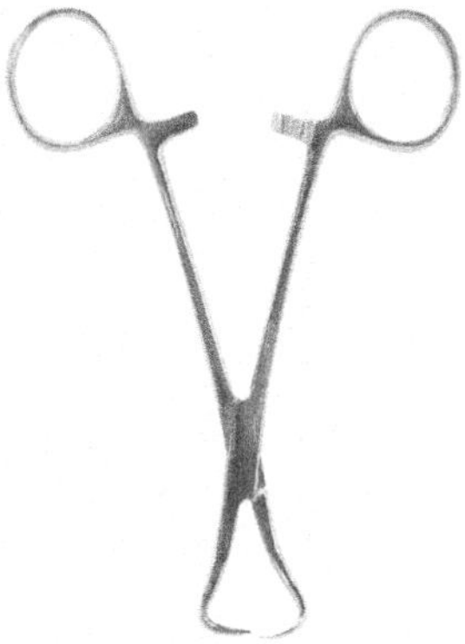

254) **Towel Clamp**

Explain What It Is Used For:

____

____

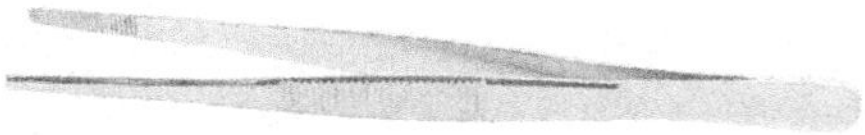

255) **Dressing Forceps**

Explain What It Is Used For (Dressing forceps have no teeth):

____

____

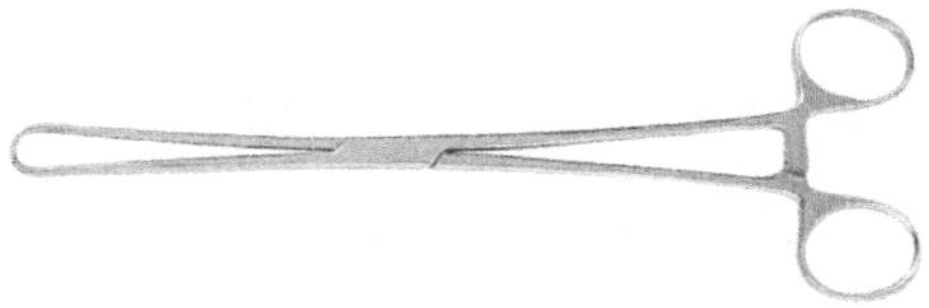

256) **Uterine Tenaculum Forceps**

Explain What It Is Used For:

____

____

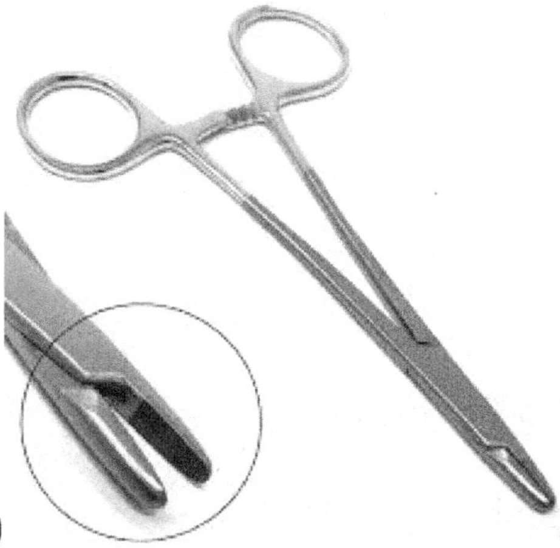

257) **Needle Holder**

Explain What It Is Used For:

____

____

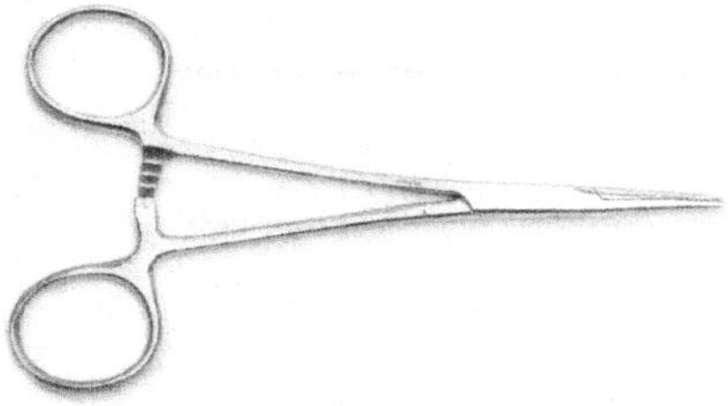

258) **Mosquito Forceps Straight**

Explain What It Is Used For:

____

____

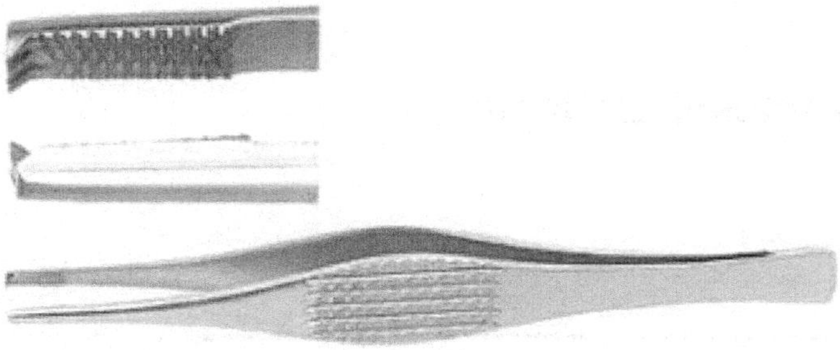

259) **Ferris Smith Pickups**

Explain What It Is Used For:

____

____

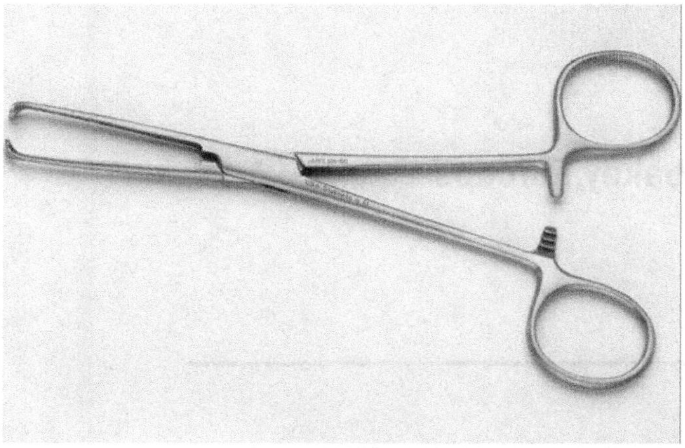

260) **Allis Forceps**

Explain What It Is Used For:

____

____

271) 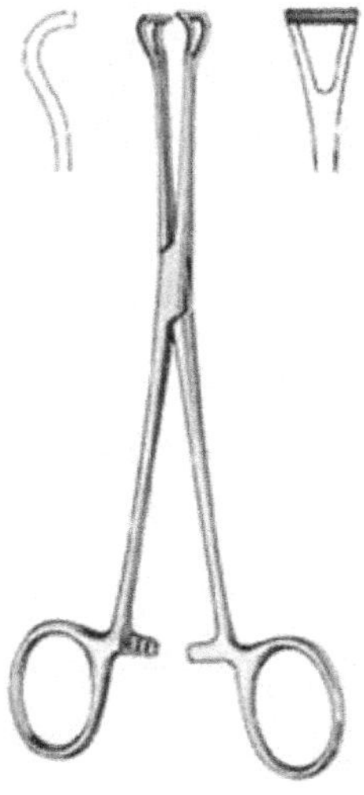 **Babcock Intestinal Clamp**

Explain What It Is Used For:

____

____

272) 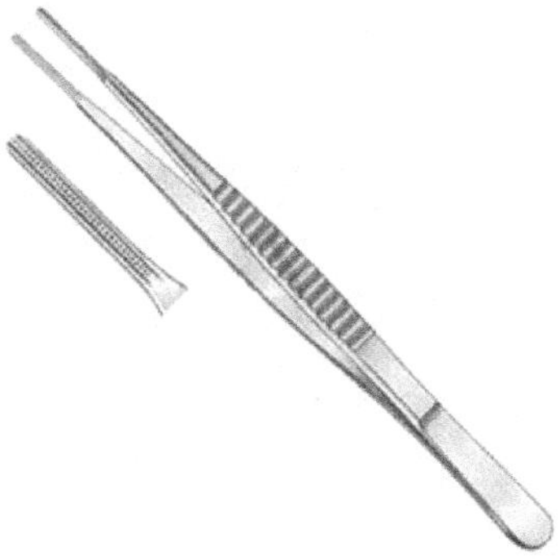 **Debakey Forceps**

Explain What It Is Used For:

____

____

273) 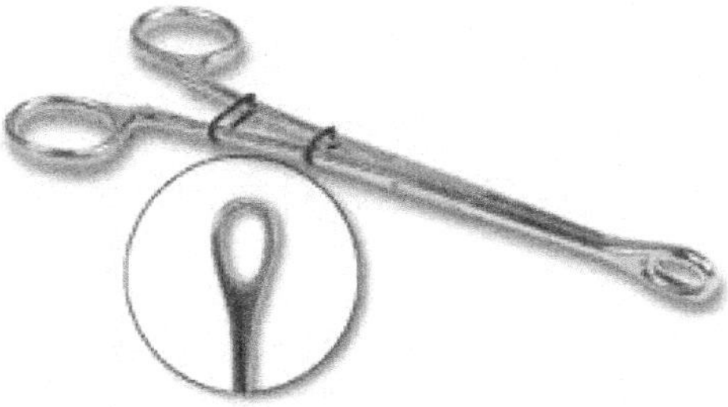 **Ring Forceps or Sponge Stick**

Explain What It Is Used For:

____

____

274) 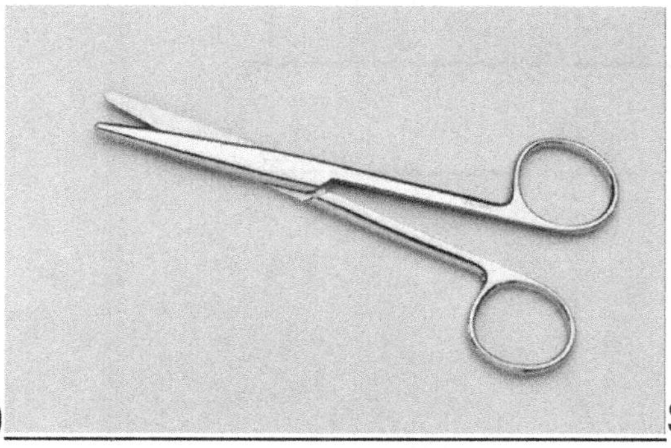 **Straight Mayo or Suture Scissors**

Explain What It Is Used For:

____

____

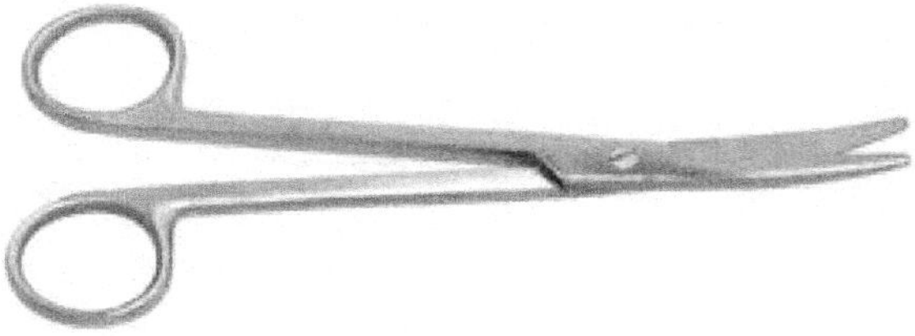

275) **Curved Mayo Scissors**

Explain What It Is Used For:

____

276) 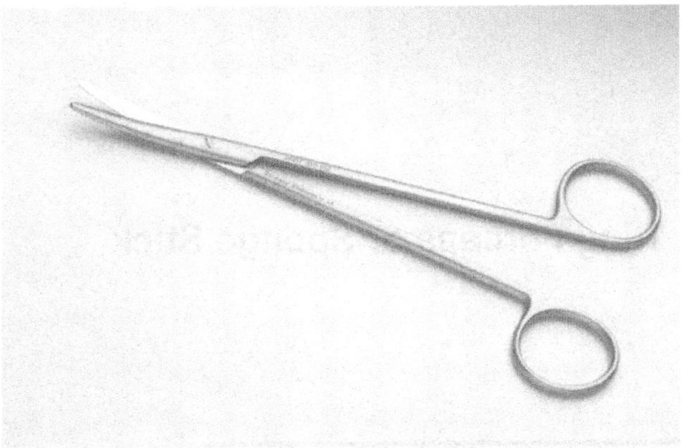 **Curved Metzenbaum Scissors**

Explain What It Is Used For:

277) 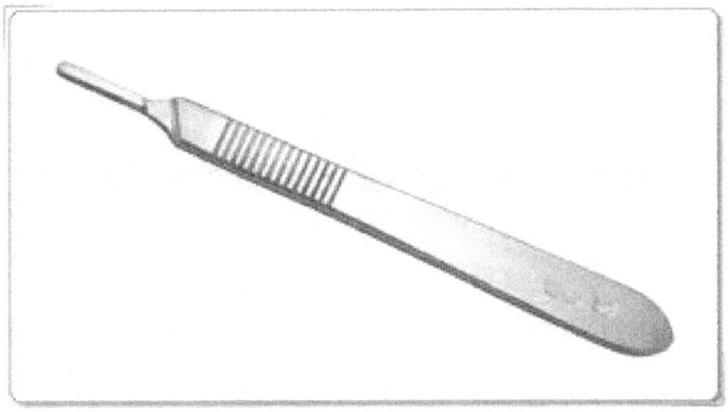 **#3 Knife Handle**

Explain What It Is Used For:

278) 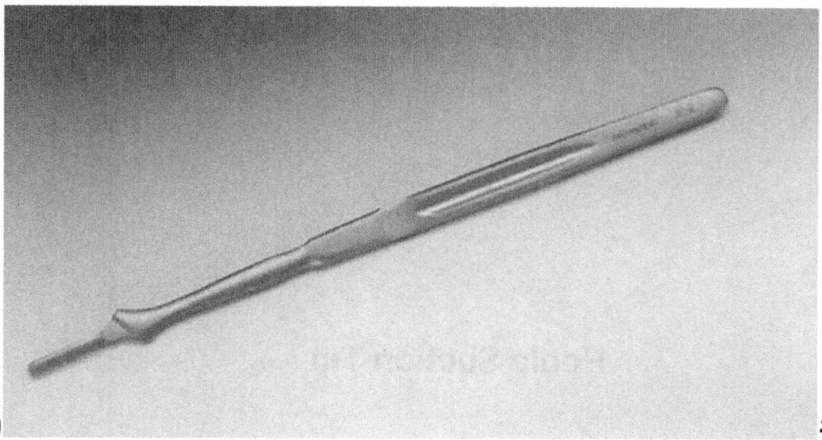 **#7 Knife Handle**

Explain What It Is Used For:

____

____

279) 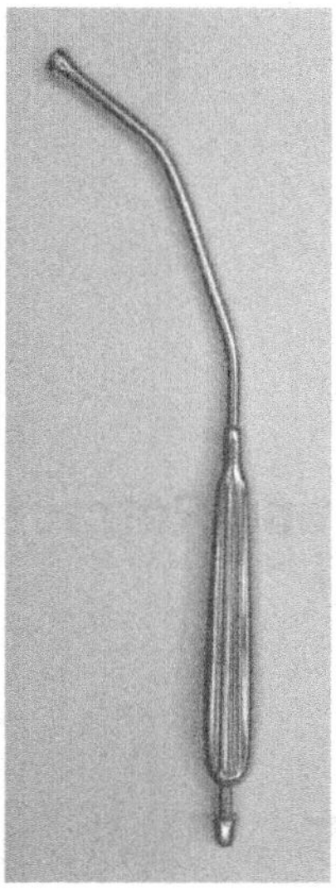 **Yankauer Suction Tip**

Explain What It Is Used For:

____

____

280) **Poole Suction Tip**

Explain What It Is Used For:

____

____

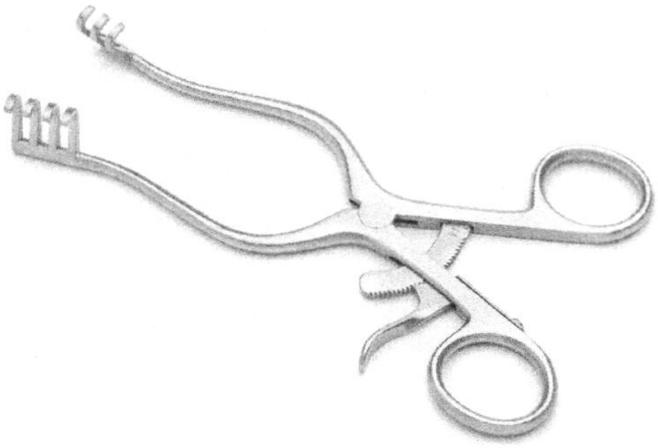

281) **Weitlaner Self-Retaining Retractor**

Explain What It Is Used For:

____

____

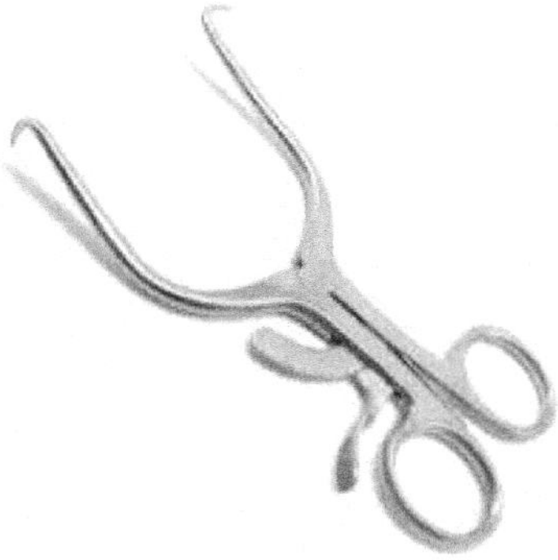

282) **Gelpi Self- Retaining Retractor**

Explain What It Is Used For:

____

____

283) 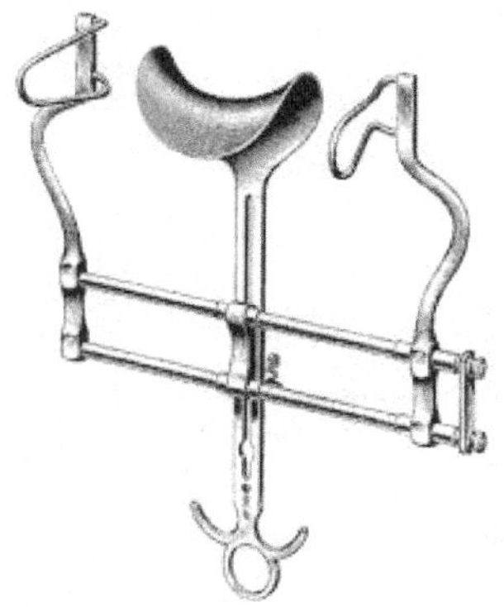 **Balfour Self-Retaining Retractor**

Explain What It Is Used For:

____

____

284) 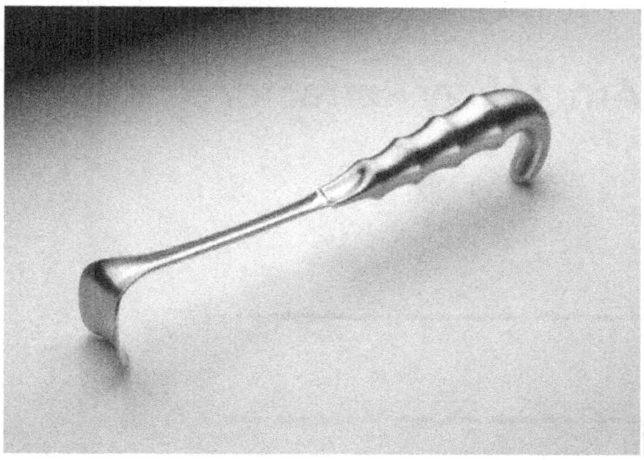 **Richardson Retractor**

Explain What It Is Used For:

____

____

285) 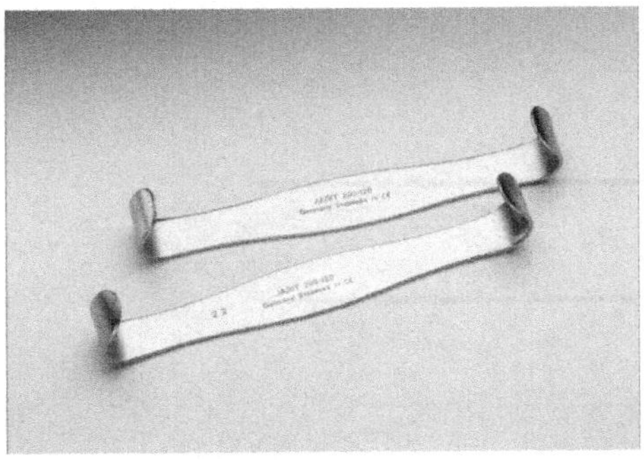 **Parker Retractor**

Explain What It Is Used For:

____

____

286) 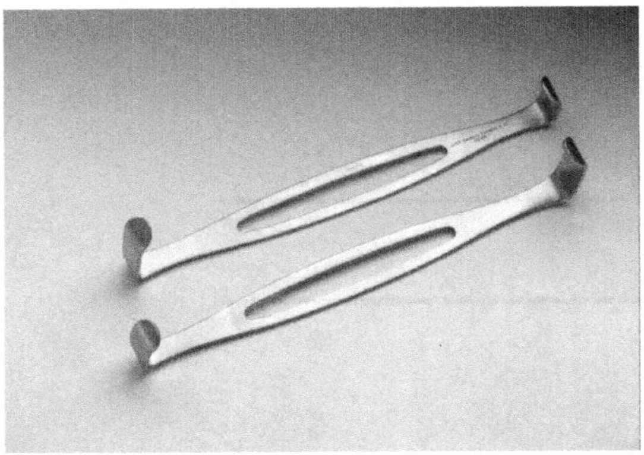 **Army Navy Retractor**

Explain What It Is Used For:

____

____

287) **Roux Retractor**

Explain What It Is Used For:

288) 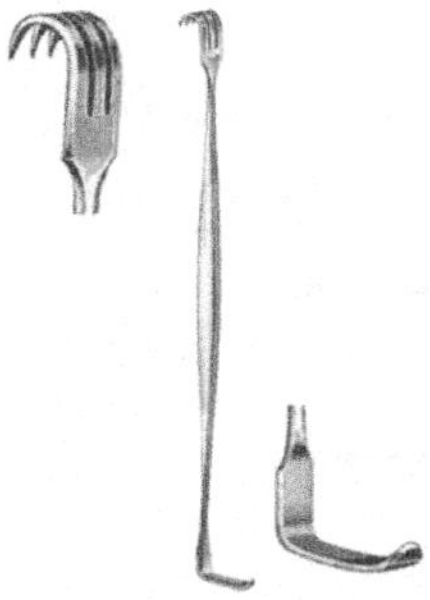 **Senn Retractor**

Explain What It Is Used For:

289)  **Green (Loop) Retractor**

Explain What It Is Used For:

290) **Harrington (Sweetheart) Retractor**

Explain What It Is Used For:

____

____

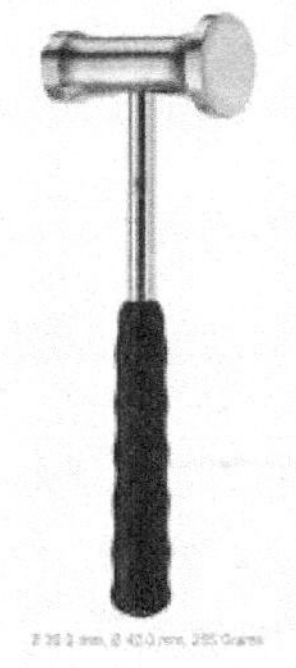

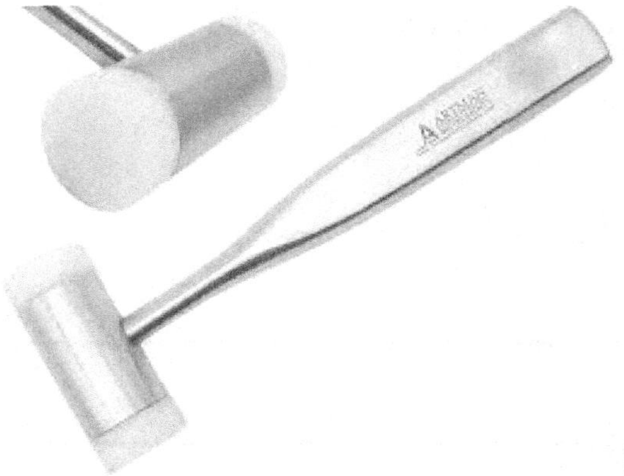

291) **Mallet**

Explain What It Is Used For:

____

____

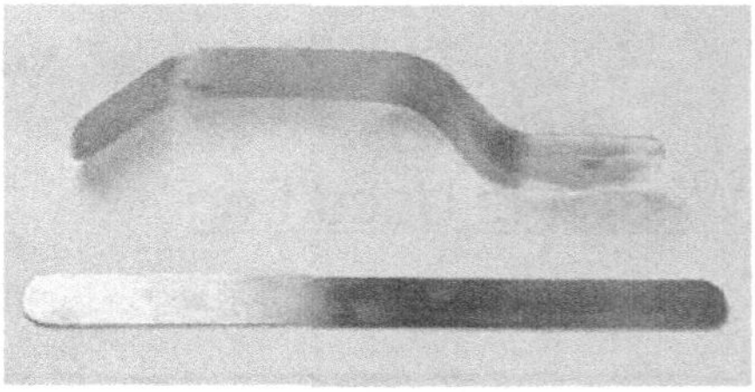

292)

Ribbon Retractor

Explain What It Is Used For:

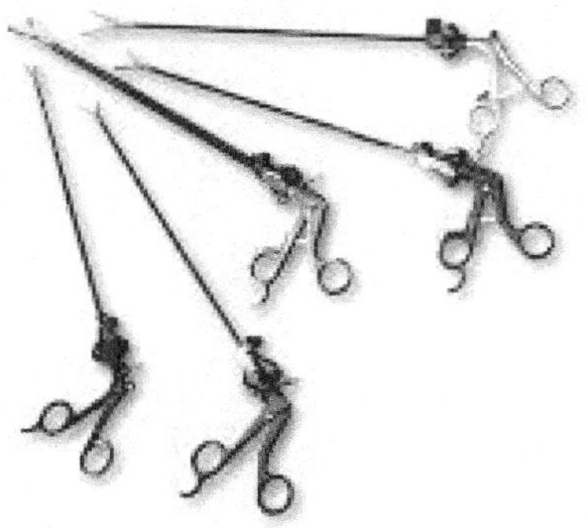

293)

Laparoscopic Instruments

Explain What It Is Used For:

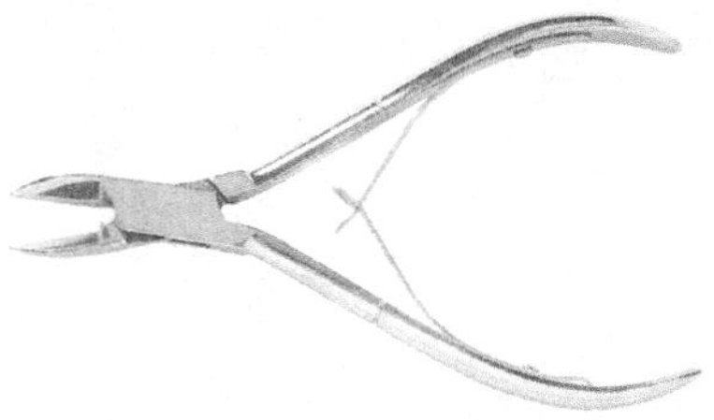

294) **Nail Nippers**

Explain What It Is Used For:

295) **Endoscope**

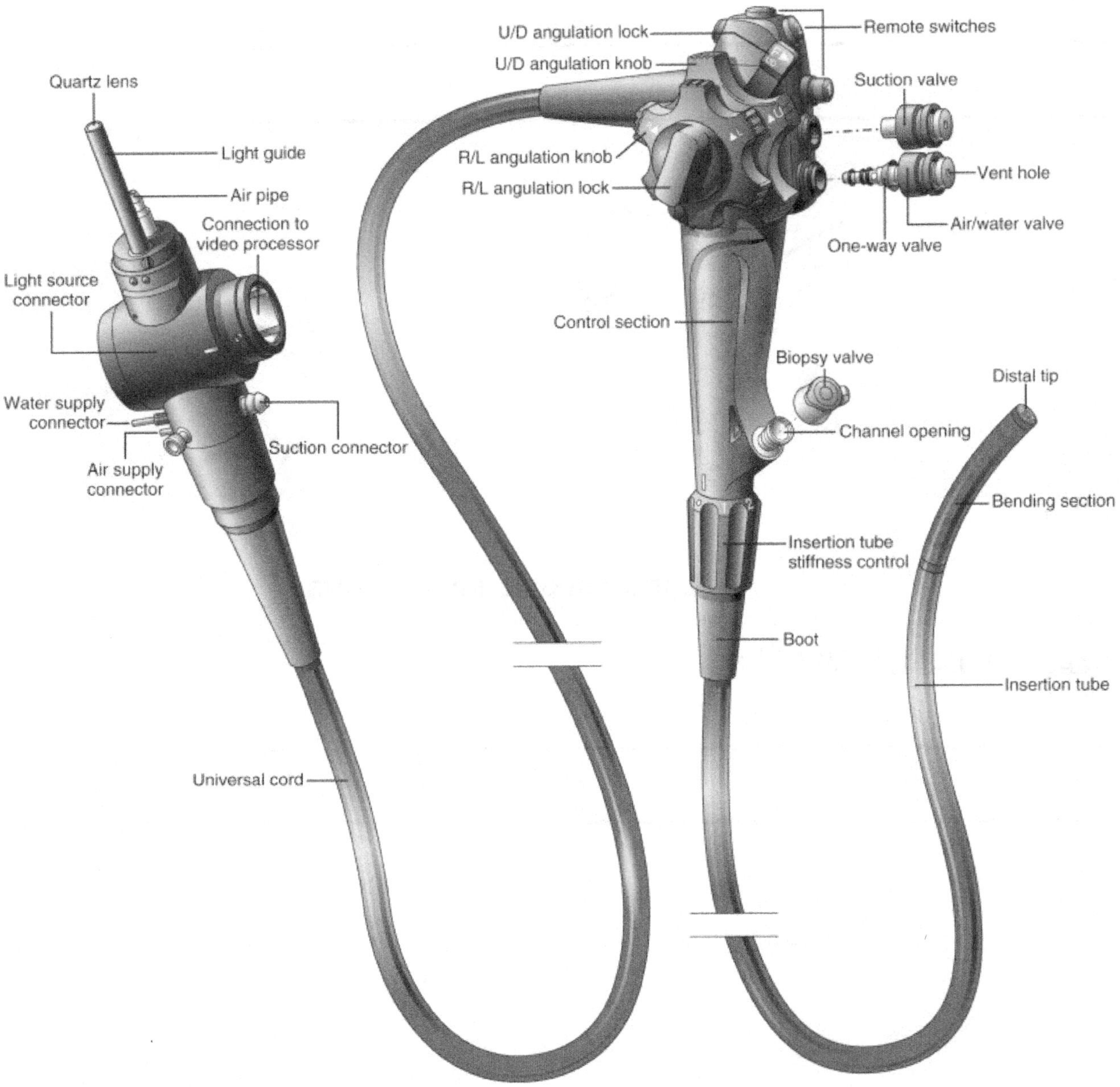

Explain What It Is Used For:

296) 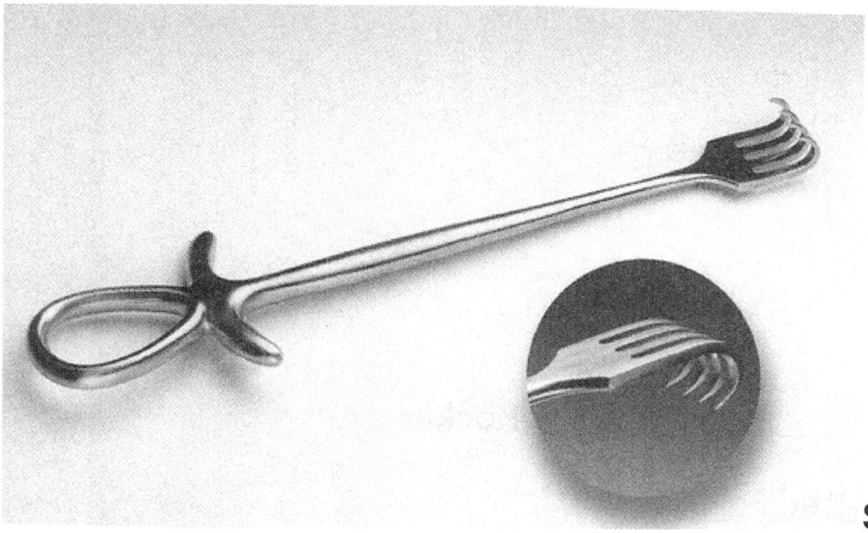 **Sharp Rake**

Explain What It Is Used For:

____

____

297) 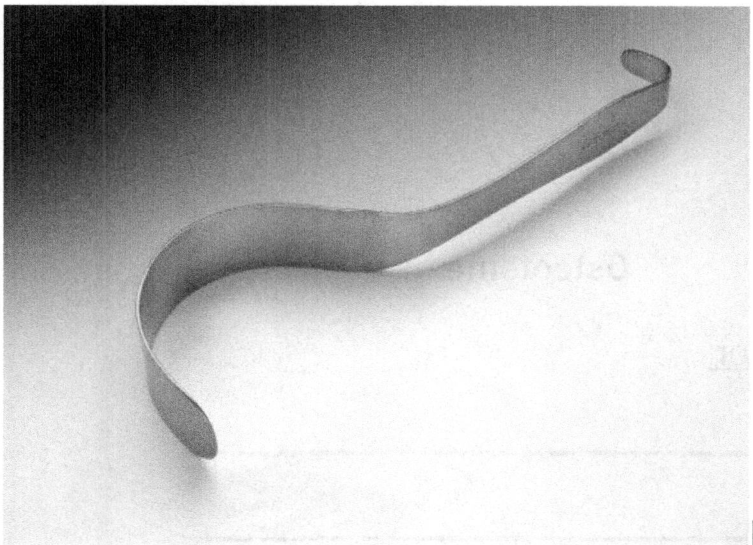 **Deaver**

Explain What It Is Used For:

____

____

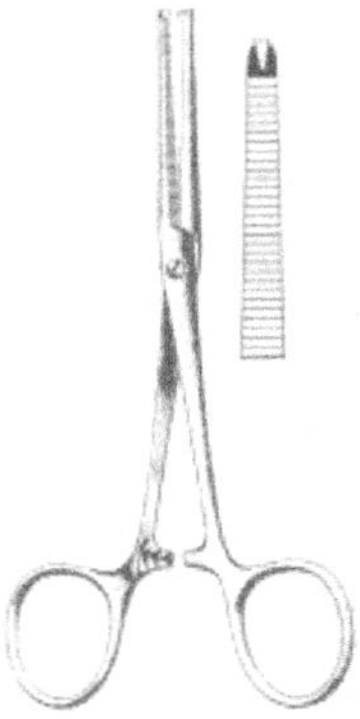

298)________________________________**Kocker**

Explain What It Is Used For:

____

____

299) **Osteotome**

Explain What It Is Used For:

____

____

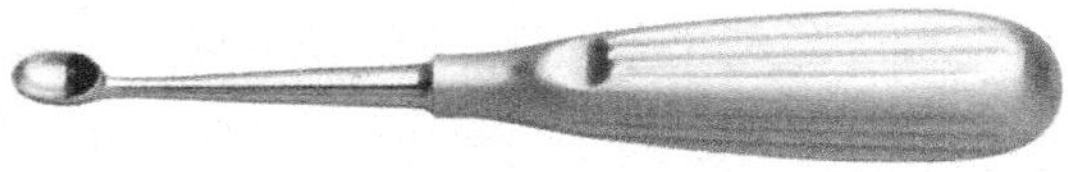

300) **Curette**

Explain What It Is Used For:

____

____

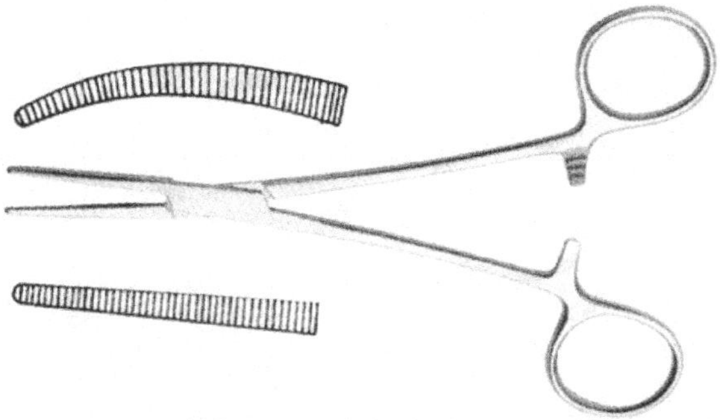

301) Curved Crile Clamp

Explain What It Is Used For:

____

____

302) Regularly using BIs to verify that sterilizers are effectively killing highly resistant bacterial spores.

a. True
b. False

Explain Why:

____

____

303) Box locks may remain closed during sterilization?

a. True
b. <u>False</u>

<u>Explain Why:</u>

____

____

304) Chemical Indicators (CI's) are used in every sterilization load and set to check for exposure to sterilization conditions.

a. <u>True</u>
b. False

<u>Explain Why:</u>

____

____

305) Define CDC:

____

____

306) Define OSHA:

____

____

307) Define AORN:

____

____

308) Define AMMI/ANSI:

309) Define SDS:

310) Define SOP:

311) Define TJC:

312) Define FDA:

313) Define Best Practice:

314) Define HAI:

315) Define MEC:

316) Define PPE:

317) Define HLD:

318) Define IFU:

319) Define Pre-cleaning:

320) Floors inside of Sterile Processing should be wet mopped only.

a. True
b. False

Explain Why:

321) The absence of microorganisms that cause disease is called:

a. Asepsis
b. Infection Prevention
c. Decontamination
d. Sterilization

Explain Why:

____

____

322) Inanimate objects that can transmit bacteria are called:

a. Fomites
b. Gram stain
c. Carriers
d. Transporters

Explain Why:

____

____

323) Gown worn in decontamination must be fluid resistant:

a. True
b. False

Explain Why:

____

____

324) Heart valves and pacemakers are an example of FDA Class III medical devices:

Explain Why This Is A **True** Statement:

____

____

325) Chemical Indicators (CI) are classified as FDA Class II medical device:

Explain Why This Is A **True** Statement;

____

____

326) The best way to transport dirty/biohazard material is in a dedicated soiled elevator:

Explain Why This Is A **True** Statement;

____

____

327) Injuries of the muscles, nevers, tendons or joints are called Musculoskeletal disorders:

Explain Why This Is A **True** Statement;

____

____

328) Neutral pH is the preferred pH for detergents used for most cleaning processes:

Explain Why This Is A **True** Statement;

329) Instrument lubrication is performed after cleaning:

Explain Why This Is A **True** Statement;

330) Thermal disinfection is performed by using Heat:

Explain Why This Is A **True** Statement;

331) The place where he two parts of a ring-handled instrument meet and pivot is called the Ratchet:

Explain Why This Is A **False** Statement;

332) Only HIGH foam detergents should be used.

Explain Why This Is A **False** Statement;

333) Surgical Site Infections are not preventable:

Explain Why This Is A **False** Statement;

334) Water quality in Sterile Processing does not matter:

Explain Why This Is A **False** Statement;

335) Wire abrasive brushes may be used in the decontamination area to remove dried on blood:

Explain Why This Is A **False** Statement;

336) Bacteria are large, single-celled organisms that are all around us—in the air, soil, water, and even inside our bodies:

Explain Why This Is A **False** Statement;

337) **Binary fission**- The typical method of bacterial reproduction in which a cell divides a cell into three equal parts.

Explain Why This Is A **False** Statement;

338) **Creutzfeldt-Jakob Disease (CJD)-** CJD stands for Creutzfeldt-Jakob disease. Is not rare and is a fatal brain disorder that causes a rapid decline in mental function and movement.

Explain Why This Is A **False** Statement;

____

____

339) **Portal of Exit:** This is how the pathogen leaves the reservoir. It is not transmitted through bodily fluids (coughing, sneezing, blood), excretions (feces, urine), or skin.

Explain Why This Is A **False** Statement;

____

____

340) **Portal of Entry:** This is how the pathogen enters the susceptible host. It could be through the respiratory tract (breathing), digestive tract (eating or drinking), breaks in the skin, or mucous membranes (eyes, nose, mouth).

a. True
b. False

Explain Why:

____

____

341) **Mode of Transmission:** This is how the pathogen travels from the reservoir to the susceptible host. It could be through direct contact (touching), indirect contact (contaminated objects), droplets (coughing or

sneezing), or airborne transmission.

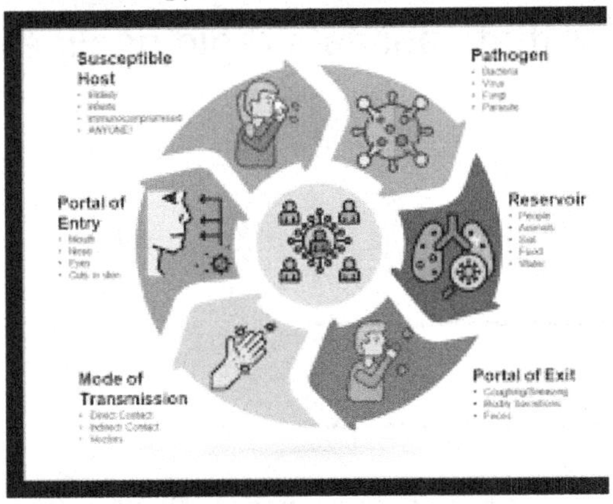

a. True
b. False

Explain Why:

____

____

342) Colonization refers to the presence and multiplication of microorganisms (like bacteria or fungi) on or within a host (a person, animal, or plant) without causing any signs or symptoms of infection.

a. True
b. False

343) The act of washing hands with soap and water or using an alcohol based hand rub.

a. Hand hygiene
b. Sanitization
c. Aseptic Technique
d. Asepsis

Explain Why:

____

---

344) Flexible endoscopes are not time consuming:

a. True
b. <u>False</u>

<u>Explain Why:</u>

---

345) Sharps containers do not have to puncture resistant as long as they have a biohazard sticker on the outside of it.

a. True
b. False

<u>Explain Why:</u>

---

346) Tissue forceps have teeth:

a. <u>True</u>
b. False

<u>Explain Why:</u>

---

347) An acceptable method of instrument identification is:

a. Laser etching
b. Identification tape

c. Powder coating
d. <u>All the above</u>

348) Semi-rigid scopes are used in urology procedures:

a. <u>True</u>
b. False

<u>Explain Why:</u>

____

____

349) Pneumatic cords are difficult to clean because they are black in color therefore soil is difficult to see:

a. <u>True</u>
b. False

<u>Explain Why:</u>

____

____

350) The process used to give instruments a mirror finish is called:

a. <u>Polishing</u>
b. Stainless steel
c. Oxidization
d. Nickel

<u>Explain Why:</u>

____

____

351) Define Borescope and explain what it is used for:

Describe in detail:

____

____

352) Technicians do not need to use a magnifying light to look for debris if they are able to see without it:

a. True
b. False

Explain Why:

____

____

353) If debris is found on an instrument, the entire tray should be sent back to decon for reprocessing:

a. True
b. False

Explain Why:

____

____

354) When using "Quad" (quaternary ammonium) wipes, drying the surface with a dry towel is permitted to speed up the dry time.

a. True
b. False

Explain Why:

355) The Prep and Assembly area is negative pressure area:

a. True
b. False

Explain Why:

356) Sterile processing (Decon) is not a restricted area:

a. True
b. False

Explain Why:

357) Clean scrubs should be worn in the prep area. If a person leaves the decontamination area to work in the prep and assembly area, technicians should change into clean scrubs before entering.

a. True
b. False

Explain Why:

358) The prep and assembly area has less than 10 air exchanges per hour.

a. True
b. <u>False</u>

<u>Explain Why:</u>

___

___

359) Airflow inside the prep and assembly area should flow into the room when the door is opened.

a. True
b. <u>False</u>

<u>Explain Why:</u>

___

___

360) The floors and walls should be constructed of materials capable of withstanding chemical agents used for cleaning or disinfecting. Ceilings and wall surfaces should be constructed of non-shedding materials.

a. <u>True</u>
b. False

<u>Explain Why:</u>

___

___

361) What is the humidity range for the prep and assembly area:

a. 60%-70%
b. <u>30%-60%</u>
c. 30%-70%

d. None of the above

Explain Why:

____

____

362) What are the minimum air exchanges in the prep and assembly area:

a. 10
b. 8
c. 4
d. 7

Explain Why:

____

____

363) Define Borescope:

a. A scope used to look inside of the lumens/channels of instrumentation and endoscopes to check for residual debris or bioburden.
b. A scope used to look into hard to reach internal cavities.
c. A scope used to remove debris from lumens/channels of instrumentation and endoscopes.
d. None of the above

Explain Why:

____

____

364) Bioburden, debris, and biofilm can not be sterilized, however hair is able to be sterilized when temperature reaches 270 degrees.

a. True
b. <u>False</u>

Explain Why:

____

____

365) Food is prohibited in the sterile processing area because:

a. It attracts insects and rodents
b. Residue left on hands may transfer to instruments
c. Impede the sterilization process
d. <u>All the above</u>

Explain Why:

____

____

366) Nail polish and artificial nails should not be worn because:

a. Potential for nail polish to chip
b. Artificial nails could fall off into tray
c. Microorganisms could be introduced to the try
d. <u>All the above</u>

Explain Why:

____

____

367) It is the supervisors responsibility to monitor the cleanliness of staff and ensure that scrub attire is dry and fit to be worn throughout sterile processing.

a. True
b. <u>False</u>

<u>Explain Why:</u>

____

____

368) Jewelry, including wristwatches and wedding rings are prohibited in the sterile processing area:

a. <u>True</u>
b. False

<u>Explain Why:</u>

____

____

369) Sterile processing technicians should not bring items such as money, electrical devices, personal items (bags/backpacks) into the area:

a. <u>True</u>
b. False

<u>Explain Why:</u>

____

____

370) Ethylene oxide (EtO) is a popular and highly used sterilization method used in sterile processing because of its safe process and virtually no harm to patients or staff.

a. True
b. <u>False</u>

Explain Why:

---

375) pH is really a measure of the relative amount of free hydrogen and hydroxyl ions in the water.

- pH range is from 0-14
- pHs of less than 7 indicate acidity
- pH of greater than 7 indicates a base or Alkaline

a. True

b. False

Explain Why:

---

376) Filters in genesis pans may be used multiple times.

a. True
b. False

Explain Why:

---

378) Relative humidity should be controlled between 30% and 60% in all work areas except the sterile storage area, where the relative humidity should not exceed 70%.

a. True

b. False

Explain Why:

____

____

379) Emergency eyewash/shower equipment must be available with unobstructed access for immediate emergency use in all locations where potentially damaging chemicals are used.

a. True
b. False

Explain Why:

____

____

380) All rigid instrument containers must be disassembled before cleaning, properly removing the filter plate and holder.

a. True
b. False

Explain Why:

____

____

381) Instrument sets should not weigh over 45 lbs each.

a. True
b. False

Explain Why:

382) If an instrument is discovered to have bioburden in the prep and assembly area, it is not necessary to send it back to decon. The debris can be removed in the prep/assembly area.

a. True
b. <u>False</u>

<u>Explain Why:</u>

383) Materials capable of holding water, such as basins, should be positioned tilted on edge and oriented in the same direction.

a. <u>True</u>
b. False

<u>Explain Why:</u>

384) Peel pack paper pouches should stand on edge in relation to the cart or shelf, with the paper side of one pouches next to the plastic side of the next pouch, holding racks or baskets specifically designed for peel packs are usable.

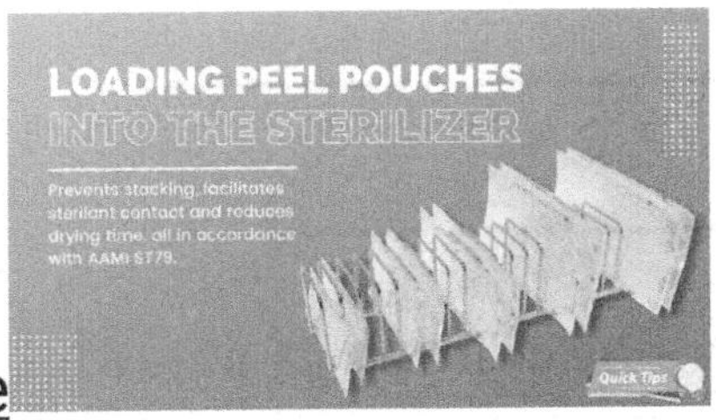

a. True
b. False

Explain Why:

____

____

385) Opening or "cracking" the door for a period of time at the end of the sterilization cycle and before the container systems are removed from the chamber allows the sterilizer jacket to continue warming the load through radiant heating from the sides, top and bottom of the chamber.

a. True
b. False

Explain Why:

____

____

386) Radiant heating in steam sterilizers compensates for heat loss caused by condensate evaporation and encourages continued drying after the cycle. However, containers made from thermally insulating materials like plastic may not absorb external radiant heat effectively. In these cases, adjustments to the drying protocol may be necessary to ensure complete drying.

a. True
b. False

Explain Why:

387) Event related sterility depends on the quality of the packaging material, the storage conditions, the conditions during transportation and the amount of handling.

a. True
b. False

Explain Why:

388) The best time to complete the manual cleaning process is within 15 minutes to an hour after the surgical procedure.

a. True
b. False

Explain Why:

389) An ultrasonic cleaner should be degassed?

a. Once a month
b. At the end of each shift
c. At the beginning of each shift
d. Everytime the water is changed

Explain Why:

390) Disposable wraps and supplies are called:

a. Consumable items
b. OR supplies
c. Patient supplies
d. Assets

Explain Why:

391) Radio Frequency Identification (RFID) tags are:

a. Tags that track instruments with real time information
b. Tags that track patient name and date of birth
c. Both A&B
d. None of the above

Explain Why:

392) Which of the following is NOT considered as a professional association:

a. OSHA
b. FDA
c. AORN
d. AAMI

Explain Why:

393) Define Preventative Maintenance:

a. Refers to identifying potential problems before they occur
b. Refers to preventing technicians to have to call maintenance
c. Refers to scheduling a maintenance service ticket
d. All the above

Explain Why:

394) What causes the gas plasma sterilizer to abort cycles?

a. Instrument not dried thoroughly- to much moisture
b. Bio burden left on instrument
c. Instrument wrapped in wrong packaging
d. All of the above

Explain Why:

395) The assembly area (prep/pack) has a dress code requirements that are:

a. Restricted
b. Unrestricted
c. Semi-restricted
d. Do not enter

Explain Why:

____

____

396) The decontamination area is a restricted area:

a. <u>True</u>
b. False

Explain Why:

____

____

397) The movement of supplies throughout the hospital is called:

a. <u>Distribution</u>
b. Case Cart System
c. Exchange cart system
d. All the above

Explain Why:

____

____

398) Ergonomic hazard is <u>not</u> a hazard found in sterile processing.

a. <u>True</u>
b. False

Explain Why:

<u>Physcial Hazard, Chemical Hazard and Biological Hazards</u>

<u>are all hazards in SPD but not Ergonomic Hazards</u>

399) Detergents are not regulated by the FDA:

a. True
b. False

Explain Why:

____

____

400) Phenolics is a disinfectant residue, when left on a surface after use, can be reactivated later by a damp mop:

a. True
b. False

Explain Why:

____

____

401) Central Nervous System consist of the brain, brain stem, and spinal cord.

a. True
b. False

Explain Why:

____

____

Know the following True Statements:

- **Robotic instruments** may **have exposed cables**
- Scissors with tungsten carbide cutting edges are usually identified by **black handles**
- **Aeration instructions** for instruments are found **in the IFU** - Instructions For Use
- **Principle for asepsis**: Know what is dirty, know what is clean, know what is sterile. Keep all these different parameters separated and remove contaminants immediately
- Glutaraldehyde and ortho-phthalaldehyde (OPA) <u>is classified</u> as a **high level disinfectant-which is FDA Class II and Semi-Critical of Spaulding Classifications**
- **Liver:** The organ which filters blood to remove amino acids and harmful toxins
- **Gallbladder function:** The gallbladder is a small, pear-shaped organ located under your liver on the right side of your abdomen. It plays a crucial role in your digestive system, primarily by storing and concentrating bile
- **The bottom shelf** in sterile processing should have a solid covering and be **8-10 inches** from the floor to prevent contamination during the mopping and cleaning process
- **The top shelf** should be no taller than **18 inches** from the sprinkler heads
- **Instrument lubrication** frequency should follow the IFU
- **Product expiration dat**e can be **located anywhere** on the package
- **Nitrile** gloves should always be worn for protection when handling glutaraldehyde
- **Latex of all types are prohibited** in the sterilization process; patients can have an allergic reaction
- **Monitoring the temperature and humidity levels** in Sterile Processing is considered **Formal Monitoring**

- The most common reason for **steam sterilization failure** is: Lack of steam contact with instrumentation in the load
- **Lipase enzymes** are used to **breakdown fatty deposits** on instruments
- **Precleaning helps to prolong** the life of the instrument
- **Asepsis** is the **absence of microorganisms** that cause disease
- **Washer disinfector racks, steam traps and ultrasonic machines** should be **inspected and cleaned daily**
- The virus that causes Hep B is **transmitted by blood**
- Muslin, twill, and a barrier cloth is acceptable for sterilization packaging, but **CANVAS** is **NOT**
- Hospital Associated Infections (HAI's) are infection that occur on or **after 3 days of a hospital stay**
- **PPE**- Personal Protective Equipment- is worn to minimize the exposure to bloodborne pathogens and other contaminants
- **Loaned instruments must decontaminated when entering SPD and before returning to the vendor**
- **Dark spots** on the visual lens of an endoscope are the result of **damaged light fibers**
- **IUSS** - Immediate Use Steam Sterilization- should not be used for implantable devices
- **IUSS** is used for urgent turnover of instruments and should not be stored on the shelf if not used
- **Leak test i**s the first step in reprocessing an endoscope
- Flexible endoscope are time consuming to reprocess
- **Surgeon identification** is not required on the sterilization package, however the description of the instrument, lot control number and identification of the sterilizer cycle is required
- **The floors** in Sterile Processing **are to be wet mopped only**. No dry mopping or sweeping
- **Adson's with teeth** are also called Tissue Forceps with Teeth
- **The staining method** most frequently used to identify the shape and characteristics of bacteria is called Gram

- **The weakest** part of a **steam sterilizer machine** is the door
- **Biofilm:** The collection of microorganisms that attaches to the surfaces and each other and forms a colony that produces a protective gel that is very difficult to penetrate with detergent and disinfectants
- Standards and regulations help set minimum levels of quality and safety
- **Gross Soil**: Tissue, body fat, blood and other bodily substances
- **20 seconds** is the duration of the time you should **wash your hands**
- **Mycobacterium tuberculosis** is a rod shaped bacteria
- Urology procedures often use **Semi-rigid endoscopes**
- **Microorganisms** reproduce by a process called Binary Fission
- **Cholecystectomy** is surgical procedure to remove the gallbladder
- **Heavy instruments** should be stored on the middle shelf to prevent injury
- **Plasma is the yellow liquid** that makes up **more than 55**% of the blood
- **Water temperature is the key source of disinfection in an automated washer**
- Aerobic bacteria requires **oxygen**
- **10 air exchanges** is required in a room that has an EO sterilizer
- When assembling instruments, heavier instruments should be placed on the bottom of the tray
- **Pituitary gland** is the gland that stimulates body growth
- Thermal disinfection is the heat that is used to kill all microorganisms except spores
- Minimally Invasive surgery has the advantage of **a shorter recovery time**
- **PAR Level System**: Inventory system that stocks supplies by pre-established stock levels
- **The DRAIN** is the coolest area in the steam sterilizer
- Remove all instruments from the shelf when cleaning it, to prevent accidental moisture

- **Antiseptics** are chemicals used on living tissue to slow the growth of microorganisms
- **Encephalopathy** is a disease of the brain
- **Exchange Cart System**: The Inventory System that uses two identical carts to facilitate supply and instrumentation replenishment
- ***Yellow test material*** is material used to test the sharpness of scissors measuring 4.5 inches or smaller
- **Quality monitoring** is the process of maintaining or improving quality outputs
- **Semi closed shelf** is a shelf with 3 solid sides
- The door of a steam sterilizer should be wiped and inspected **daily**
- **Viruses** have no means to move on its own
- **Pasteurizers** disinfect using **heated water**
- **The brain center of a cell** is called the **Nucleus**
- **Peel pouches should be placed on the edge, paper to plastic for steam sterilization**
- Formal communication is an example of **Coaching**
- **Spreading rumors** is an example of **informal communication**
- **Eye wash stations should be checked weekly** (not daily) to ensure they are performing according to the IFU's
- **Tracking individual instruments** is important for the following reasons: locate missing instruments, knowledge of where set is located at all times, and knowing what instruments are in what specific set
- **Biological (Bi's) monitoring devices** are **not** considered as a physical monitor, however temperature control monitor, operating pressure gauges and timing records are
- **EO (Ethylene Oxide)** cartridges should be stored in a ventilated, flammable liquid storage cabinet that is exhausted to the outside and kept away from heat, sparks or sunlight
- Sustainability is designed to reduce harm to the environment
- The Sterile Processing area has customers from different parts of the hospital such as clinic areas, Emergency department and Labor and

Delivery, however The Operating Room **(OR) is the major focus for sterile processing personnel**

You've made it this far – you've conquered the study guide and now it's time to shine! Head over to HSPA or CBSPD and ace that national sterile processing exam. I believe in you! This is your moment, your calling. This exam is just the beginning of an amazing journey.

Your future in sterile processing is bright and full of possibilities! There might be challenges along the way, but remember that you are strong and capable. You've got this! Push through, persevere, and you will achieve great things. The rewards will be worth every effort. Go out there and make your dreams a reality!

Renita Hoof

Clinical Director and Instructor, ST, CRCST, CHL, CIS, CER, MRCST

Notes:

Made in the USA
Monee, IL
09 May 2026

49821537R00083